When You Have
Volume

By Ryusho Jeffus

Copyright 2019

Myosho-ji, Wonderful Voice Buddhist Temple
611 Vine3 St.
Syracuse, NY 13203 USA

License Notes

ISBN: 9781686208140
Imprint: Independently published

Quotations from the Lotus Sutra:
The Lotus Sutra
The Sutra of the Lotus Flower of the Wonderful Dharma
Translated from Kumarajiva's version of
The Saddharmapundarika-Sutra
Third Edition
by Senchu Murano
Copyright 2012 Nichiren Shu

Table of Contents

When You Have Great Joy
Volume 1

by

Ryusho Jeffus

Forward

What follows is a collection of essays, Dharma talks, and lectures given on various occasions. Unlike the essays found in Lotus Path, these are generally 1000 plus words with many several thousand.

The subject matter is wide ranging, covering subjects from a Buddhist perspective. It is my belief that there is nothing in life that we are unable to find Buddhism and apply our Buddhist teachings.

In my writings and speeches I strive to give encouragement in one's practice of Buddhism in daily life. I do not think that the doctrines of Buddhism lie outside of our everyday experiences.

I hope you will find these writings to be of value as you live your Buddhist life.

With Gassho,
Ryusho Jeffus
Kansho Shonin

More Books by Rysuho Jeffus:

Lecture on the Lotus Sutra

Lotus Sutra Practice Guide

Important Matters

Daily Lotus

Incarcerated Lotus

The Magic City

The Physician's Good Medicine

Lotus Path Vol 1 & 2

Contemplating Disease

King Wonderful Adornment

Lire du Sutra du Lotus

Cité Magique

Le Bon Remède du Médecin Habile

Roi Ornement-Merveilleux

Cuestiones Importantes: Sutra del Loto, Fé y Práctica

Disertaciones sobre el Sutra del Loto

Wait With One Mind

February 23, 2014 Dharma Talk

"The good omen I see now is like that of old.
This is an expedient employed by the Buddhas.
The present Buddha is also emitting a ray of light
In order to reveal the truth of the reality of all things.

Manjusri said to the multitude.

All of you, know this, join your hands together,
And wait with one mind!
The Buddha will send the rain of the Dharma
And satisfy those who seek enlightenment."
Lotus Sutra, Chapter I

These lines appear at the conclusion of Chapter I and in them Manjusri is reassuring the great assembly that the Buddha will reveal a great teaching. Manjusri encourages those present to wait patiently with their minds focused together on listening and preparing to receive a teaching, which will be like nourishing rain.

I selected this passage as my final subject for the last Dharma talk in February and the last talk in this series about Chapter I because of the phrase 'wait with one mind'. I have been doing some reading lately about trends in our modern lives and the influence of technology on the way we think and live. Because we live in a world in which we are almost constantly turned on and connected we are increasingly loosing the ability or practice of waiting, being patient, and remaining focused.

We frequently think that this has lead us to be more productive because while we are waiting for one series of steps in a project to be completed we can begin or resume another project thus jumping from one thing to another, all in various stages of completion and perhaps even covering various subjects requiring different solutions. Our minds trick us into thinking that because we are not idle we are therefore getting more done. But this fractured, or splintered fragmented approach to living is actually robbing us of focus and creativity as well as mental energy; at least that is what some early research is now revealing.

While it may only take the body a few minutes to change tasks it actually takes the mind many minutes to first find a way to disengage mental focus from what was previously being expected of our brain. This disengagement is sort of like putting away thoughts but doing so in a way that will facilitate rapid recall and resumption, which are not things that our minds have a lot of prior evolutionary experience. So our mind is being expected to 'wind down' in ways it might not be the best suited for.

This 'winding down' also needs to take place even as the brain is expected to 'wind up' with a new project, which may or may not be something that had been worked on previously. This takes a significant toll on the brains overall ability to sustain this kind of activity as well as the energy to be creative and accurate. What generally tends to happen in research is that the brain tends to mediocrity even without the awareness of the subject.

So, our brain hides from us that while we think we may be more productive our productivity actually becomes less effective and the results are compromised in the long run.

Loosing focus or the ability to truly focus and concentrate is a common problem for many in today's world. Yet there is no less demand to be focused, especially if we want to have a feeling of being fulfilled and living a meaningful life. While we as a society are loosing our ability to focus and concentrate, which we are replacing with multi-tasking, society as a whole is experiencing greater dissatisfaction with life. Meaning and purpose are being cited increasingly as something that people miss the most in their lives, yet previous generations did not as frequently.

There is a strong connection between focus and concentration and feeling purposeful. It is almost logical there would be that connection. If the brain is focused then the whole of the body is also and there is a unity not just of purpose and function but also of action and energy. When we are less focused we are less mindful and less aware of the entire goings on in our body and what it is experiencing.

When we sit in meditation and chant the Odaimoku we can begin to practice this focus and concentration, but it requires effort. There may be times when our chanting will be distracted and our thoughts all over the place. There is nothing abnormal about this. Over time though, as we become aware of what our mind, our body is telling us we can learn to listen and let go. Chanting is a chance to practice focus and concentration. We can wait with one mind as our life enriches itself with the sound of our chanting the sacred title of the Lotus Sutra.

Our daily practice is an activity of joining our hands together and waiting with one mind so that we can nourish our lives with the rain of the Wonderful Dharma of the Lotus Flower Sutra. I hope that you all will continue to strive in your practice. I also hope that you are increasingly able to bring the truths of Buddhism into ever greater parts of your lives. When we can fully integrate Buddhism into all aspects of our lives, we will be in greater harmony and receive greater benefits from our efforts of faith, practice and study.

Treasures We Do Not Seek

April 20, 2014 Dharma Talk

Good morning thank you for attending the temple this Easter morning. Even though Easter is not a Buddhist holiday there is much in the spirit of the holiday we can appreciate. Today I would like to share with you a connection I make with one part of the Easter story and the Lotus Sutra.

As you know I work as a chaplain and in my work here in Charlotte I am frequently, almost entirely, called to spend time with Christians. Not being raised in a particularly Christian family there is really much of the religion I was not aware of prior to my training to be a chaplain. One of those things was the idea of Saturday in the story of the crucifixion and resurrection Christian celebrate at Easter. Today I would like to talk about Saturday.

In a way the idea of the uncertainty of Saturday after crucifixion is an appropriate metaphor for many things in our lives. In case you don't know what I am talking about, Saturday was a time of great uncertainty for those early followers of Christ. They had just witnessed their spiritual teachers death the day before. For my Christian friends who may read this, please forgive me if I make some doctrinal errors.

On Saturday those early disciples of Christ who were not yet called Christians were probably very upset, grieving the loss of their teacher just the day before. For us as moderns who know the outcome of the story it is easy to forget how uncertain these people may have felt. They did not know what the future would hold for them. There may have even been the thoughts of giving up, of being spiritually adrift.

In Chapter VI of the Lotus Sutra the arhats say to the Buddha "We have obtained innumerable treasures although we did not seek them." When we read this it is easy to understand both the delight and the acknowledgment of the benefit of the treasure of an improved life condition resulting from our Buddhist practice.

Yet in the time before we see the benefit of our Buddhist faith and practice it isn't easy to be able to claim any delight in benefits not sought after. There are times in our practice when we may face some serious troubles, when moving forward seems terribly hard if not down right impossible.

I imagine Saturday might have been such a time for the followers of Christ. How do you proceed when the worst has happened? How do you go forward after you have lost a loved one? How do you get up the next day after you have been diagnosed with a terminal disease? How do you have a morning cup of coffee when you need to rush to the hospital to be with a sick or dying loved one? How do you find joy when the worst possible thing has happened to you? How do you praise the benefit of the Lotus Sutra when you see no benefit in the moment?

Sometimes it seems our religious beliefs call on us to do the impossible. Yet isn't it really the other way around? When we are faced with the seemingly impossible isn't it our religious or spiritual beliefs the very thing we can rely upon to get us through?

Sometimes we view events as tests of our religion or our faith when really we might better think of it as we have difficulties as a natural part of being alive and religion is what can give us direction in those moments. When you look around at every thing in life think about just how difficult it is to even be alive. Living is a treasure no matter how brief or turbulent it is. Right now there are literally hundreds of dead canker worms on my front porch, there are hundreds more plastered all over the sides of the house. These were living beings that struggled and did not make it. Life is a struggle, but we as humans have an expectation that it will be roses and easy.

We look at resurrection or enlightenment as if this is how every day should be, as if somehow we should expect lives of ease and comfort. We forget too easily the Saturdays of our lives. We forget the years of struggle the Buddha engaged in so he could be awakened. We forget just how tenuous life really is.

Life is the treasure and our awareness of this is the treasure we sometimes are most unaware of and take for granted. This is the first treasure we should celebrate. When we can fully celebrate the treasure of life and realize that Saturday is a key part of that treasure we can be opened to the other treasures in our lives. When we live with a sense of entitlement to lives of ease we delude ourselves and thereby miss the moments of just being alive.

I wish you a joyous day and life as Buddhist, as Christians, as Jews, as Muslims, and as the many other ways of expressing and living as spiritual beings.

The Gathered Assembly

February 2, 2014 Dharma Talk

Good morning, thank you all for joining today either in person at the temple or via our live stream on the internet. Today we celebrate the Lunar New Year as well as Setsubun. Before I get into my Dharma talk I would like to take a moment to introduce to you Madoka Shiota a student from Japan. Madoka will be staying here at the temple the entire month of February while she studies to improve her English attending classes at Queens University. Her visit here was arranged by the Nichiren Shu Overseas Bureau as part of a program to give opportunities for Japanese priests and relatives an opportunity to experience life in the United States. We sincerely welcome Madoka and pray her stay here is both enjoyable and educational.

As I mentioned to day we celebrate the start of the Lunar New Year and Setsubun. The Lunar New Year used to fall more closely in time with spring, now at least in China and Japan and a few other places it occurs in February on the third. The custom of Setsubun we celebrate is the tossing of soybeans. In old times people would clean their houses in preparation for the start of the Lunar New Year. They would then invite a priest to come and perform purification blessings on the dwelling chasing away any demons so the New Year could be fortune filled and problem free. As the soybeans are scattered it was customary to say 'Oni wa soto fuku wa uchi' which roughly translates as demons out and fortune in. Now days the ritual takes place at the temple and fills in for the personal ritual done at home.

The tradition in some places is to eat the number of soybeans that represent the age you will be this year plus one. The plus one is so the age will be in line with how old you would be if you were Japanese, because the Japanese count things slightly differently than we do, but I won't go into that in detail right now.

Today I would like to talk to you about the assembly gathered together at the start of Chapter I in the Lotus Sutra. I know for me it is still very difficult to read through the list of people who are present while the Buddha sits quietly in meditation. It is much easier to read it in the Chinese and actually has quite a song like quality that we miss out on in English.

According to Nichiren the size and variety of people in attendance is unlike any ever before in any of the sutras previous to the Lotus Sutra. In this assembly we not only have a large number of people we also have a large variety of beings, both human and non-human. Why is this important and what significance does it have for us as modern practitioners of the Wonderful Dharma of the Lotus Flower Sutra?

I would like for you to take a moment and consider your list of friends, not Facebook friends but real life friends. I am guessing the list of real life friends is much smaller than the Facebook list which probably includes people you haven't actually ever met. Among your list of real life friends I wonder how many of them are very much like you are? Are your friends similar to you in economic wealth or poverty? Are your friends more similar to you in looks and age? Are your friends more similar to you in political beliefs, or even religious beliefs? How much variety is there among your friends, and could all of your friends easily get along with each other? How much of an ambassador are you among your list of friends?

Generally speaking people are friends mostly with others who are most alike in some way. It is the rare person who can have a list of friends who are greatly diverse and even rarer still is the person who seeks to bring a diverse friendship group together at the same time and in the same place. Frequently if the friends are diverse people keep their friends separated.

Thinking about all the ways we segregate ourselves, and how difficult it is for many people to get along, it is significant that the assembly gathered for the Buddha was peaceful, diverse and large. I suppose some modern mega-churches might approach the size and diversity of the assembly at the Lotus Sutra, but only in the human realm.

As to the size of the crowd Nichiren points out that never before had such a large gathering of people assembled to hear the Buddha preach as had gathered for the Lotus Sutra. To him, and to others, this is significant because it shows the importance of the teaching. Remember too, the assembly actually increases in size when later on in the sutra the Buddha calls back all of his emanations and they arrive with their entourages.

Thinking again about your own life and the friends you have, the number of people who would come to assist you if you were in trouble, or the number of people who would come to your funeral, or birthday party. That number may be large or it may be small and it may even depend upon what you are asking your friends to do. How much diversity is there in your friend list of those who would come to your aide if you were in trouble, and what is the size of that list?

Many people today surround themselves with either virtual friends, that is friends who don't really exist in their everyday physical world, or they surround themselves with people who are most like themselves. Being around people who are most like you is frequently advice given to people in search of AA groups to overcome drinking addictions. But as Buddhist we should be comfortable around diversity in all the ways it can be classified. Through our practice of cultivating our lives and understanding ourselves we can develop lives that can cultivate and understand and relate to very different kinds of people.

Also developing, cultivating, and nourishing real time face-to-face friends is hard work but the benefit to one's personal well being is priceless. It is easy to seek pleasurable things, and sometimes not being around people may seem to be the most pleasurable experience. But we have become addicted to seeking pleasure and avoiding discomfort in all areas of our lives, and personal interactions is no exception. We are too easily adverse to unpleasant or difficult things, even the unpleasant and difficult things about ourselves.

Interacting with others and increasing our exposure to differences can serve to help us develop and grow as Buddhists. It is also certainly advantageous if we wish to share the Dharma with others.

Think about the assembly gather around the Buddha and then think about the assembly gathered around your own life. As we conclude the final observance in our New Year celebrations perhaps you can consider making a determination for the remainder of the year to increase the number of real time friends and the diversity of your intimate list of friends.

Let me close by wishing you a happy New Year may it be one of peace, happiness, good health and good fortune.

Praising the Buddha

March 9, 2014 Dharma Talk

Good morning to you all, thank you for joining with me today to celebrate the Lotus Sutra by reciting portions of Chapter II and Chapter XVI as well as harmoniously chanting the sacred title. Today is the first day of Daylight Savings Time here in the United States. For most of us the next few days or even weeks will be challenging as our bodies adjust to the change in time. I know I am one of the group for which it takes several weeks to make the adjustment.

As I was thinking about this it reminded me of something I had read a short while ago

> *"The things you do often create the things you believe."* McRaney, *David (2013-07-30). You Are Now Less Dumb: How to Conquer Mob Mentality, How to Buy Happiness, and All the Other Ways to Outsmart Yourself*

Each of us will over the course of the next few days, thanks to the necessity of following social conventions gradually adjust our bodies and our minds to becoming in rhythm with the new time. By doing the same things daily in the new time schedule we will eventually "believe" in the new time and we will forget the old time. In other words because we are forced into making the adjustment eventually we do make that adjustment.

The book I quoted is an interesting book, which explores the function of the mind delving into understanding why we think the way we do and some of the universal principals that we all seem to follow even unknowingly.

In Chapter II there is a section which talks about the merit to be obtained by doing various practices such as making images of the Buddha, making offerings to the Buddha including beating drums, by offering flowers and incense, and by expounding the Dharma to others. Not only do we gain the merit of the Buddha by doing those things ourselves but we also benefit from causing others to do the same.

> *"Those who respectfully offered*
> *Flowers, incense, streamers, and canopies*
> *To the image or picture of the Buddha*
> *Enshrined in a stūpa-mausoleum;*
> *Or those who caused men to make music*
> *By beating drums, by blowing horns and conches,*
> *And by playing reed-pipes, flutes, lyres, harps,*
> *Lutes, gongs, and copper cymbals,*
> *And offered the wonderful sounds produced thereby*
> *To the image or picture of the Buddha;*
> *Or those who sang joyfully in praise of him for his virtues;*
> *Or those who just murmured [in praise of him],*
> *Have already attained*
> *The enlightenment of the Buddha."*
> *Lotus Sutra, Chapter II*

By doing the various practice of Buddhism, such as reciting the sutra, chanting the Odaimoku, meditating, making offerings, and teaching others are all acts which further strengthen our own belief according to science.

The really interesting thing which science has discovered is that the belief that is nurtured by doing then leads to becoming.

These things then influence you to become the sort of person who owns them. McRaney, David (2013-07-30). You Are Now Less Dumb: How to Conquer Mob Mentality, How to Buy Happiness, and All the Other Ways to Outsmart Yourself

In other words our practice, engaging in the various practices the sutra teaches us, enhances our faith, which then enables us to transform our lives into being those things we practice.

Faith, practice and study are the three cornerstones of Buddhism, which have been so since the very beginning. What the Buddha understood more than two thousand years ago today science is proving.

I encourage each of you to carry out your Buddhist practice faithfully day-in and day-out so that you are able to transform your lives into the lives of Buddhas and reveal your vast inner potential.

Let us together attain Buddhahood and enable countless others to do the same.

> *"Those who bowed to the image of the Buddha,*
> *Or just joined their hands together towards it,*
> *Or raised only one hand towards it,*
> *Or bent their heads a little towards it*
> *And offered the bending to it,*
> *Became able to see innumerable Buddhas one after another.*
> *They attained unsurpassed enlightenment,*
> *Saved countless living beings,*
> *And entered into the Nirvāṇa-without-remainder*
> *Just as fire dies out when wood is gone."*
> *Lotus Sutra, Chapter II*

Most Famous Mother in the Lotus Sutra

May 11, 2014 Dharma Talk

Good morning to all who are present either here at the temple or viewing the live stream or even those who only read this blog. Happy Mother's Day to all the mothers out there, and Happy Mother's Day to my mother who died in 2002.

The most famous mother in the Lotus Sutra is actually a demon. Kishimojin is not the only mother in the Lotus Sutra, she is however the most famous one and a statue of her is usually present in Nichiren Shu temple, ours is on a side altar left of the main altar. Kishimojin is a manifestation of Hariti from India who is the deity representing fertility, childbirth, and childhood diseases. She has both a positive attribute and a negative one as well.

In Eastern mythology just as in Greek mythology the deities were not always without some negative characteristics. The deities were not simple beings who only represent good or evil as is the case later on in Western European mythology where many of the lesser qualities are frequently ignored or not spoken of.

This is actually rather fitting to consider as we celebrate this special day we set aside to celebrate our mothers. Every one of us has a mother, but not all of us are comfortable celebrating our mothers. For many the relationship with their mother is complicated, encompassing both good and bad emotions. Over time some come to a greater appreciation of their mother as they learn to set aside the negative memories. And over time some never reach that healing and continue holding a negative image of their mother.

Mother's too frequently have complicated relationships with their children. It isn't always that a child brings joy to the life of the mother.

Relationships are always complicated though we may wish them to be simple.

Kishimojin is portrayed as an ogress or a non-human in Japanese iconography. Throughout the ages in her various representations in different cultures she is not always depicted as such. The influence of the Lotus Sutra on Japan and Japanese culture perhaps is the reason why Kishimojin is depicted in such a way.

According to mythology Kishimojin is the mother of many children, the number varying in different tellings, but in the Lotus Sutra she has 10 children who are raksasa, or devil, and they receive their nourishment by their mother stealing human babies to feed them with.

I had often wondered how this negative image of Kishimojin stealing human babies came about, there must have been some reason for this idea. As it turns out it is the negative aspect of childhood disease that is the root of the idea of Kishimojin stealing human babies.

In the story the humans make pleas to Shakyamuni Buddha to do something to save the children. The Buddha steals one of Kishimojin's babies and hides it under his robe. When Kishimojin discovers her missing baby and after looking everywhere she goes to the Buddha greatly distraught. The Buddha produces the baby and explains that while she has so many children humans usually only have one or two babies so as much as she missed one of many so too humans miss even more the loss of one of so few.

Repenting her ways Kishimojin then vows to protect practitioners of the Lotus Sutra and to no longer steal babies to feed her own. In Chapter XXVI Kishimojin and her children make vows to protect those who uphold the Lotus Sutra. This is why we set aside a special place for a statue of her.

"Anyone who does not keep our spells
But troubles the expounder of the Dharma
Shall have his head split into seven pieces
Just as the branches of the arjaka-tree [are split].

Anyone who attacks this teacher of the Dharma

Will receive the same retribution
As to be received by the person who kills his parents,
Or who makes [sesame] oil without taking out worms [from the
sesame],
Or who deceives others by using wrong measures and scales,
Or by Devadatta who split the Saṃgha."
(Lotus Sutra, Chapter XXVI)

As I mentioned in the beginning not everyone has a good relationship with their mother, there may be many complicating factors in our memories of our mother. Not everyone has had a good experience with their mother through their lifetime. And not every mother had good experiences with their children. It may not be possible to forgive either our mother or for mothers their children. The hurts may be too deep and too severe.

My own relationship with my mother both when she was alive and even in death is one of those complicated ones. Neither she nor I were perfect in any way. We were neither all good nor all bad. That is most commonly the way of much of our lives. Yet what are we to do with the negative stuff, for the good stuff is usually easy to accept.

I believe that no matter what it is possible to shift our thinking to one of possibilities. Through our practice of Buddhism and the Lotus Sutra it is possible to change our lives in such a way as to open up new ways of either viewing the past or of reinterpreting previous experiences. For some whose mother is no longer living it can be difficult, that is the case with me. There is no one living to sort things out with, and so the work is left to the individual.

Sometimes we are left only with the possibility of moving on, of not being help captive by the past. Sometimes we may be able to come to a realization that no thing is either all good or all bad, even though is it frequently easier to hold on to the bad stuff. It may take learning how to less tightly hold on to the negative and more firmly grasp the sometimes tiny bits of good.

Today on this Mother's Day it is my prayer that we can all come to celebrate our complicated relationships with our mothers while also realizing that we too are complicated individuals and our mothers may have also complicated relationships with us.

I cannot imagine the difficulty of nor the joy of motherhood. I can only be in awe of the efforts of being a mother. Even my mother showed devotion to being a mother even if it manifest in ways that were sometimes hurtful to me. Today I would like to remember those efforts of nurturing, rearing, providing, protecting, sacrifice, pain, and suffering that my mother gave.

May the Fourth be With You

May 4, 2014 Dharma Talk

Good morning, I hope everyone is doing well today and has had a pleasant weekend so far. I don't know about where you live but here in Charlotte yesterday the weather was beautiful. My dog and I walked over eight miles yesterday, played with my new chickens and even had time to read and cook out. While I was out walking I spent a lot of time talking to neighbors out working in their yards or also out walking.

Today is Star Wars day May the fourth and that is how I titled today's Dharma Talk as a take off on "May the Force be With You." Now I must be honest here, I am not a big Star Wars fan so there is much in the plot and story I don't remember. I have seen all the episodes but cared little enough to commit them to memory. I saw the first episode, though it wasn't really the first part, in a theatre in Hawaii. That is about all I can recall of the movies other then of course some of the main characters.

In today's Dharma talk I bring this up because I wanted to talk about our struggle with our personal practice and achieving enlightenment. As we engage in our Buddhist practice of the Lotus Sutra frequently we will be faced with many challenges, that we can be assured of because the Buddha actually predicts this many times in the course of his delivery of the Lotus Sutra.

Obstacles to our practice can make their appearance in many forms. Sometimes these hindrances may be our job interfering because of time required to work or even a hostile supervisor opposed to Buddhism. The interference might also come from family life when we might not have sufficient time to engage fully in our practice. Other times there may be various other obstructions that arise causing us to abandon or slack off in our practice.

While all of these and many more may serve to limit our practice it is ultimately up to our own mind as to whether we succumb to them and abandon the path to enlightenment. In the story of Star Wars, if I have my facts correct, we could say that Anakin Skywalker gave in to the forces of evil and became Darth Vader, for us that would be giving in to the forces of Mara and abandoning our practice altogether.

As we learned Darth Vader, Anakin Skywalker, is actually the father of Luke Skywalker, and as Darth Vader he tried to influence Luke to joining forces with the Sith and going over to the Dark Side. Luke however overcame the temptation and coercion and the final betrayal of learning his own father was Darth Vader. We could say that Luke beat back the forces of Mara in his life and stayed true to the Force.

We too most assuredly will face challenges to our practice however it is solely up to ourselves as to whether those difficulties win over and cause us to abandon our practice and fail to attain enlightenment.

> *"Your merits cannot be described even by the combined efforts of one thousand Buddhas. Now you have defeated the army of Māra, beaten the forces of birth and death, and annihilated all your enemies. Good man! Hundreds of thousands of Buddhas are now protecting you by their supernatural powers."* Lotus Sutra, Chapter XXIII

I hope that you will continue your practice even in the face of great adversity. Realize the ultimate obstacle we all are faced with, the one that has the greatest power over us is nothing other than our own minds. It is our mind that determines whether we will achieve enlightenment. Our own mind is where the greatest struggle against Mara or the Dark Side takes place. Every time we overcome our own self doubt or our desire to quit we are victorious over Mara and we advance our own enlightenment.

As you go through this week and the days of your life I hope that you will keep this in mind. In closing I wish you great merit and "MAY THE FORCE BE WITH YOU!"

Knowing the Past and Changing the Future
March 16, 2014 Dharma Talk

Good morning, thank you all for joining with me this morning to celebrate the Lotus Sutra and practice according to the instructions given to us by Nichiren Shonin. Continuing with my weekly reflections on the Lotus Sutra I offer you this from Chapter II.

> *"All things are devoid of substantiality.*
> *The seed of Buddhahood comes from dependent origination."*
> *Lotus Sutra, Chapter II*

Originally I had planned to go in a different direction reflecting on this passage, however just this morning I received an interesting question by email and decided to respond.

The question posed is roughly this: why do we have to suffer from unskillful causes in our past if we made those causes in ignorance, not knowing the skillful way to act?

The idea of karma being a result of some previous action is an incorrect concept of Western understanding of Buddhist teachings about karma. This is probably due in part because of the way it was translated but also because we as humans have a tendency to want to blame something or someone for what is happening to us. There is a desire to wish that we were not some how responsible for our actions, and that we are in some way a victim.

At any rate let me state simply karma is not what is happening to us. Karma is not the effect. Karma is what we are doing now. Karma is the causes we are making in this very moment. Karma is the cause we make and not the effect we receive.

Your karma is not what is happening to you; instead it is what you are doing in this very moment. Karma is how you respond to situations and events in your life. Karma does tend to be repetitive because we generally tend to respond in certain ways, which we have learned or developed. Those repetitive ways of responding generate similar effects. For example if we are prone towards anger and respond angrily to every event in our lives then we will continually receive the same results. The results are not our karma but our responses are. The two are not easily separated but by changing our responses to events in our lives is changing our karma and that intern changes our results.

The idea of dependent origination is simply that nothing comes into existence or exists independent of something else. So too our lives did not come into existence without the necessary sperm from a man and an egg from a woman, even if we were artificially produced in the so called test-tube. The egg and sperm gave us our genetic background from which we have grown. Our very life and existence is dependent upon many individuals both known and unknown to us.

There is no way possible to completely separate ones self from others. Also there is no way to separate this moment from the last or the next. There is no moment that arises independently of a series of previous moments.

So this very moment contains all of the previous moments and in this moment we are able to practice Buddhism and affect all of our future moments. It is because of this connection to the past causes that we are able to practice Buddhism now. In a way our enlightenment exists only in this moment you could say, because it is in this moment that we awaken to the true nature of reality, which is this dependent origination.

To wish we were somehow devoid or not accountable for our previous causes, however they were made, is to in effect wish we would never become Buddhas. I believe that enlightenment is partially if not completely about continually awakening to awareness and understanding about our current behavior in response to those countless unrealized and unaware causes we made in the past.

The theory in education is that each successive level of achievement is based upon the foundation of previous learned lessons. It is the rare individual that is able to attempt calculus without some previous understanding of basic math principles. So too our enlightenment is based upon not being perfect and not having lived a flawless life. If we had lived a perfect or flawless life then we would no longer be seekers and as the theory goes we would have left the stream of rebirth.

Let me say that it does seem rather naïve to think that in life we should be absolved of any action because we plead ignorance. We don't always treat ourselves that way nor do we treat each other that way. We may concoct a story in our minds that says we treat ourselves and others fairly and in all instances forgive ignorance but I believe that is a myth we delude ourselves with. Society says 'ignorance of the law is not excuse' and guess what, that is pretty much how we all operate. There are even people of other religions who teach that just because you were ignorant of some savior or teaching does not get you out of hell.

Buddhism doesn't teach that you are a victim of your ignorance, instead it says that regardless of how you arrived at where you currently are in life your happiness exists in this very moment and the way to that happiness is by changing your karma, your actions. It also teaches that the truth is, because of your ignorance you are actually able to become a Buddha, because all of those past causes you made got you to this very point enabling you to practice Buddhism now.

The final question in the email asks how can we learn from our past mistakes if we do not remember them. Because of the dependent origination and the continuity of past, present, and future we need only look at our lives in this very moment to begin to see what our previous causes were. Is that easy to do, is it pleasant to do, it is neither easy nor always pleasant. However, in reality the most important practice, and even the Buddha said this, is not about looking over your shoulder to the past but simply examining your present and acting according to Buddhist teachings. After all, the past we have no way of undoing except by changing our present thereby ensuring a future of happiness.

I hope you will consider carefully what your karma is; what actions you are engaged in. Karma is what you are doing now, not what you did in the past. Chanting Odaimoku, the Sacred Title Namu Myoho Renge Kyo is the most effective way to begin to change our lives and attain enlightenment in this very moment.

Thank you all again for today, and I wish you a happy and joyful week ahead.

Illuminating the World

February 9, 2014 Dharma Talk

"Thereupon the Buddha emitted a ray of light from the white curls between his eyebrows, and illumined all the corners of eighteen thousand world in the east down to the Avichi Hell of each world, and up to the Akaistha Heaven of each world." Lotus Sutra, Chapter I

In this selection we are made aware of the phenomena the assembly present at Mount Sacred Eagle witnessed the Buddha perform. Not only were these places illuminated but also those assembled were able to saw the Buddhas of those worlds and the people in those worlds carrying out Buddhist practices. This is quite a wonderful thing to consider.

Not only did the ray of light illuminate far away places it also made it possible for people to see the great distance and witness people in those worlds doing Bodhisattva practices.

The really remarkable thing about this is we all have an equal capacity to do this same thing. We are naturally awed and perhaps inspired by the Buddha being able to do such wonderful things. In our awe are we oblivious to our own ability?

I think there are two ways to consider this ray of light. One is the fact that it illuminates other worlds, the other is reveals the practices of others. Thinking about our very own lives, it might be interesting to consider what our personal beam of light is doing.

How is your life illuminated and how are the lives of others in your environment illuminated? It is possible to shine the light of enlightenment on the things that surround you. I am not sure if you have ever played around with colored lights, perhaps you have.

When I was in the Marine Corps for a brief while I lived in a barracks that had individual four man rooms. In one of my friend's room he had painted everything in the room red with blue speckles. The only light in the room was a red light, which made the red painted object almost vanish, and the blue speckles turn almost black and were really apparent. It was a rather 'trippy' effect, which was the intent. In white light we are able to register all of the colors available to the unaided eye. However, under colored light the effect is certain colors are no longer visible.

As we go through your daily activities I wonder what is the color of the light that illuminates the world around you? What is there in your environment that you are unable to see because you have a filter over the light emitting from your life? Depending upon the filter you observe life through what you witness and experience will be affected. If you have an angry filter on then everything will fit the pattern of seeming to cause you to be angry. But in reality it is the way you are reacting to the experiences you are a part of but are only seeing a selected spectrum of events.

We can choose which filter to observe our environment with. Our Buddhist practice even allows us to witness our environment through the lens of the Buddha, which enables us to see and experience the Buddha land that surrounds us. You might say that Buddhist practice lifts all the filters through which we make observations, assessments, and judgments about our experiences.

Now thinking about how the beam of light illuminates so many realms when it is emitted from the Buddha's brow, we can ask ourselves who do we illuminate the world around us. Do we bring the light of enlightenment into other people's lives or do we cast a shadow?

When we have interactions with others do we light up their lives or do we cause darkness to descend upon them? Think about what the feelings you project onto people. We have a choice as to whether when we look at people we wish them good or we wish the ill will. We can even influence the response of their life with ours.

Being able to see the Buddha in others with the illumination of Buddha in our lives is a wonderful experience that is possible for us. It is possible to bring great joy into the lives of other people and enable them to awaken to their own Buddha potential.

It isn't always necessary to tell people about Buddhism and your Buddhist practice. When someone recognizes the joy they experience because of your presence, or the kind words you share with them, or the concern you express for their life and well being, when the experience that compassion, they automatically praise the Buddha in you, even if they are unaware of it.

By praising the Buddha in you it awakens the Buddha in them, which will manifest at some point in the future. We are practicing the Buddhism of sewing when we plant such seeds as those. Nichiren said the Lotus Sutra practice in the ages after the death of the Buddha is the practice of the Buddhism of sewing.

It is possible for us to see into the lives of others to witness their sufferings, their pains, their disappointments, their frustrations, their joy and their happiness. We have the ability to open our lives up to the connections with other people which will enable us to share the results of our Buddhist practice with others in a life-to-life way.

Consider the way in which your life illuminates the world around you, and consider the manner in which you illuminate the lives of others. We all have unlimited potential, we only need to awaken to it and manifest it in our lives.

I hope you will ponder this as you go about your daily activities. I wish you well in this upcoming week.

Getting Back to It

January 5, 2014 Dharma Talk

It is possible to make a case for Fall being the time to mark the beginning of one year and the end of an old one. The crops have grown and been harvested, the growing season is completed. The fall begins and we prepare ourselves for winter slow down, possibly even hibernation. Some scientists have made a claim that our bodies have a built in rhythm that goes counter to our current Gregorian calendar making January an unnatural time to begin. Regardless, we are stuck for the present with the cycles we have and we need to make the best of them.

Between the beginning of the Gregorian New Year and the Lunar New Year is a good time to engage in a period of reflection and intention setting for the upcoming year of activities. While the cycle of the New Year may be an easy demarcation for this it is an activity and practice we can constantly engage. Let me now offer to you a possible framework over which you can construct your own personal reflection and renewal.

How much of your life is actually yours and how much of it is someone else's? When was the last time you thought about the things you do the things you think, what you like and what your opinions are? If you are thinking, and doing things the same as everyone around you it might be a sign that your life has lost it's individuality, and you have become a life that is being lead. How freely are you able to do what you want to do or think what you want even if you are the only one doing it and it goes contrary to what your acquaintances are doing? It isn't wrong to be like others, as long as it is our intention and not their intention, which is being followed. Are you at the present the kind of person you thought you would be 10 years ago? If not, what happened to that person? It may be there were some necessary changes in the 10 year vision, or it may be that the vision has become obscured. Now is a good time to reflect on what you need to do to get back on to your own path and not the path of others.

Sometimes one of the most difficult things to do is to let go of something that does not really exist. We are very clever animals capable of constructing believable illusions to support a desire to avoid confronting the realities of life. There may be things you were wrong about; choices you made that really were not wise. It is sometimes extremely difficult to admit to and let go of those choices. We are sometimes more gifted with the ability to construct a false reality than we are with admitting to a mistake. Living in the false reality or with the mistake long enough does not make it any more true. The really interesting thing is the correcting of the or mistake or the adjusting of the perception to what really is actually takes less energy and yields greater happiness in the end. But the fear is what keeps us locked into the energy depleting and happiness robbing cycle.

Following that is the opening up of other possibilities and the changes we can make. Until we let go of our false realities we will never begin to invest our creativity into other choices. As long as we are spending our energies constructing believable illusions we will not ever begin to make plans to actually change the things that caused us to enter that cycle in the beginning. So while the letting go of the illusions and admitting the need to change can be painful initially, it will quickly yield to the hope and joy of opportunity of change.

Oscar Wilde once said; "We are all in the gutter, but some of us are looking at the stars." Cultivating a mind that tends toward hope and gratitude requires just that, cultivation. As you engage in the effort of reflection and renewal do so with a mind of hope and gratitude. Get into the habit of gratitude. Plant the seeds of happiness so that happiness will actually bloom in your life. Our Buddhist practice is a good way to nurture this and at the heart of Buddhism is gratitude. We are grateful to our teachers, to the teachings and to the support of fellow practitioners.

Personal integrity isn't something we often think about or discuss in Buddhism. Yet every time you do something good, something valuable, either for yourself or for someone else even when no one is looking or when no one will know you are practicing a personal integrity. When you had a choice and you chose to do good for no other reason than to do go you were true to yourself and your beliefs. So when the next time you question your worth or your value or your contributions remember those times when you practiced personal integrity. Those personal decisions set you apart and create outcomes, which matter to you and to the universe. At the time of reflection it is equally important to bring up and consider your personal integrity.

As much as we may like to think life is in our control, in fact there is little we do actually control; more frequently is a series of likely predictions. We might use the language of tomorrow I will get paid, or tomorrow I will do some thing, but the reality is those are predictions since any number of unforeseen events could occur to change the predicted future activities. I do believe that the closer we live to this very moment and the less we live far out into the future the greater our ability is to make wise choices in the moment and to deal with the things that occur to upset our lives. When you are in the moment and not the past or future you can go more easily with the flow of life. The surprises in our life can be wonderful opportunities to learn new ways of being, but only if we are open to them and not fighting.

Finally after all of this reflection it is also important to renew and now is a good time to bring up some of your good ideas and make a plan to do something about one of them. This time is like a bridge that can take you to the other shore, the shore of a new life. You have a choice to cross the bridge and make the changes and begin anew working on the things that are meaningful and life giving, or you can turn back and return to the ways of life that are not so nurturing. Even if you consider yourself very happy in this moment there is always that bridge to cross to even greater happiness and growth. A life that is not growing is actually shrinking. Enlightenment is a process not a destination. How is your process going?

Concentrating the Mind

February 16, 2014 Dharma Talk

Good morning, thank you all for joining with me today to recite portions
from the Lotus Sutra and chant the Sacred Title, Namu Myoho Renge
Kyo. Today is Sunday, which for many people in the world, but not all,
is the traditional beginning of a new week. I hope today you are able to
make good causes for a successful week. Chanting Odaimoku and reciting
the sutra are excellent ways to make such good causes.

As I have done every Sunday this month today I will offer some further
reflections on Chapter I of the Lotus Sutra. Every month I'll focus every
Sunday Dharma talk on one chapter. In the past two Sundays I have talked
about your personal assembly of people whom you associate with and
gather into your life. I have also talked about how we illuminate the world
around us. Today I want to spend a little time talking about controlling
our minds, concentrating, and dealing with distractions.

> *"I also see some Bodhisattvas*
> *Giving up wanton pleasures,*
> *Parting from foolish companions,*
> *Approaching men of wisdom,*
> *Controlling their minds from distractions,*
> *And concentrating their minds in hills or forests*
> *For thousands of billions of years*
> *In order to attain enlightenment of the Buddha."*
> *Lotus Sutra, Chapter I*

I am not sure if you are anything like me, perhaps not. I do admit to
struggling with maintaining focus and concentrating my mind. I struggle
with the constant pull of various communication devices as well as modes
of communication. I have tried to put some limitations or even restrictions
in place, though they haven't always been met with success.

I understand from my own first hand experiences the difficulty of maintaining control over all the technology that we have allowed into our lives. In some instances it isn't simply a matter of our own choosing, but also of others in our lives.

I am currently reading a book titled: <u>Manage Your Day-to-Day: Build Your Routine, Find Your Focus, and Sharpen Your Creative Mind</u> by Jocelyn K. Glei as part of the 99U Book Series. In this book, which is a collection of short essays by various people from various fields, I have come across interesting observations which I think fit nicely with our Buddhist practice and also tie in to todays talk.

Technology of all types plays an ever increasing role in our lives. Technological devices allow us to accomplish quickly and efficiently all sorts of things, which were unimaginable previously. There are few areas of our lives where technology hasn't impacted in some way. In fact it is so pervasive we hardly even think about its presence. Television is one example, as is the radio, which we probably don't even give a second thought or even think of it as technology. However television and radio, even for as long as they have been around are new in the history of mankind. My parents were not early adopters of the modern technology of television and so I recall when we first got a television set. For many young people today the computer has always been present in their lives as well as the cellular phone.

And so, with the pervasive presence of all sorts of technology I wonder how many of us are even aware of our use. How much thought goes into our turning on the television, or the computer and checking email, or browsing the web? How many of us consider mindless usage of the devices around us?

How many of us actually get up, make our morning beverage in complete silence or in conversation with others in our house, and do all of this with no TV, no Internet, no Radio, just the sounds of humans or those from nature outside?

A function of concentrating the mind is to be aware of the mind itself. Yet how much of our lives are lived completely unaware of what it is we are doing and the reasons for doing it. Concentrating the mind is to work against and overcome mindlessness. There is nothing inherently wrong with technology and the use of the devices that aid us in our lives. The devices are neither good nor bad, it is our use and the role we allow them to assume that determines their actual value.

To seek out wisdom and abandon foolish friends does not only mean our relationship with people. Our relationship with all the things in our lives are worthy of examining to determine if they contribute value and enhance our lives leading to enlightenment.

It might be useful if we each consider our actions throughout the day taking time to examine what it is we are doing, why we are doing it, and in what way does it contribute not only to our immediate happiness but to our long range goal of enlightenment. Even as we chant we should be mindful of how easily our mind is distracted, or even pulled towards the other things in our lives that stimulate us.

Let us all not become distracted from our own lives, turning over control and mindlessly engaging in activities that do not positively impact our connection to Buddhism and enlightenment. From today refocus your life on the important goal of attaining enlightenment and also enabling others to have joy in their lives.

Chanting the Odaimoku

January 19, 2014 Dharma Talk

Good morning. Thank you to all of you here in the temple and to those of you who have joined in to our live video stream. Also, thank you to those who will read this at some other time. Thank you for your efforts to practice the Dharma thereby enabling you to attain enlightenment, thereby establishing your happiness as well as the happiness of those in your environment.

In Nichiren Shu our main practice is chanting the Sacred Title of the Lotus Sutra, the Odaimoku of Namu Myoho Renge Kyo. In addition we recite portions of Chapter II and Chapter XVI the two most important chapters in the Lotus Sutra. These two chapters are the heart of the sutra.

When we chant the Odaimoku it is as if we are reciting the entire Lotus Sutra, which is contained in the title Myoho Renge Kyo. Why is chanting the title equal to chanting the entire sutra? It is because the title of a writing is the summary of that writing. Just as if I were to say to you Moby Dick a variety of images, memories, feelings are called to mind. The same may be said of other books such as Harry Potter, Gone With the Wind, or countless others you may be familiar with. The ease of the recalling of memories depends greatly on how familiar you are with the contents of the book.

Because we may not be intimately familiar with the contents of the Lotus Sutra, the sound of Namu Myoho Renge Kyo may at first be simply foreign sounds. That is why it is important to study the Lotus Sutra so we become as familiar or more so than we are with the contents of any other book. And yet, the value of chanting Odaimoku is not dependent upon our intellectual understanding of the contents of the sutra, because the value of chanting lies in our devotion fundamentally.

The word Namu which is appended to the title Myoho Renge Kyo signifies our devotion to the contents of the Lotus Sutra. I believe that this single word, two characters as written in Chinese, symbolizes our heart. The degree with which we devote ourselves to living in accord with the teachings of the Buddha is a manifestation of our actual devotion. For it is not possible to really believe something at the core of one's life and then live contrary to the teaching. This is not living a life of integrity.

Our chanting then serves the purpose of focusing our mind and our heart towards the teaching of Myoho Renge Kyo while in our daily life we strive to actually manifest the teaching through our actions. So our chanting infuses our life with the Myoho Renge Kyo. You could think of it like the plucking of a string sets that string in motion and produces a sound, think of a guitar or a piano, or harp. And so it goes the more you chant the more your life plays the beautiful music of enlightenment.

Also Namu is manifest in our actions so it is important to have our actions match our words or else the Namu is hollow and purposeless. The Namu we say with our voice needs to match the Namu that is manifest in our lives. And so Namu then is on the one hand something we say and on the other something we do. Having the two perfectly in accord, having them in harmony is the ultimate fulfillment of devotion. And it is that devotion which activates the Myoho Renge Kyo that already lies at the core of our lives.

Now I would like to talk a little about devotion, because that is one of the meanings of Namu, or Namaste the Indian word from which Namu derives. When I first began chanting I was told that I could get anything I wanted if I chanted the Odaimoku, but that in order to get that thing I had to really apply myself to diligently chanting. It wasn't enough to only chant once in a while, or occasionally, or just a little. As you know I am not a big advocate of using the clock to gage how much you should chant. That being said however it is important to chant consistently and an amount that mirrors your devotion and your objective.

I was talking with some Buddhist monks from Vietnam one day and their opinion of Americans in their practice of Buddhism is most are lazy and insincere. The reason they felt this way was because Americans seemed to think that practicing occasionally or infrequently was sufficient. Even those who were slightly more dedicated spent less than an hour a day practicing Buddhism. The thought that was laughable to think it possible to achieve any benefit from Buddhism much less the lofty goal of enlightenment.

When you think about it almost everything that most people want they are willing to spend more time doing other things than attaining enlightenment. Watching an hour of TV, or playing video games, or many other things are much more time consuming and acceptable for most people. The idea of spending one hour or two hours a day in devotion to the thing we claim to be the most important thing in life seems unrealistic to most people, and yet they claim their devotion.

Matching your actions with your thinking is critical. Yes there are times when you will be unable to spend an hour or two hours, but if this practice is important to you if you really mean what you say, then you will find the time. Some things may need to change, but that is what attaining enlightenment is all about. Changing your life at its very core, changing the fundamentals of your life is the surest way to accomplishing your true happiness. This is the promise of Buddhism, your enlightenment.

We say Namu, but do we live Namu, we say Myoho Renge Kyo, but do we live Myoho Renge Kyo? We are still in the early days of this year, I encourage you to take a critical look at your life and see if your practice is really in line with your expectations. I suggest that you strive to make the Lotus Sutra the center of your life. In your mind try to cultivate an attitude that the Myoho Renge Kyo is the most important thing and chanting the Odaimoku is the thing that means the most to you and it comes first.

I have told this story before but I think it is worth repeating. When I first began to practice this Buddhism I was in the Marine Corps, this was back in 1969. I went to my senior, my mentor in this faith, to ask for some instruction about how to find the time to chant, go to meetings, and back then we went to meetings every single night and they were two hours long. I asked how is it possible to do my Marine Corps stuff, and all the other things and have time to chant an hour a day. My mentor asked me what was the first thing I did when I got back to the barracks at the end of my shift. I said, well I sit down on my footlocker, smoke a cigarette, take off my boots, and relax, and so forth. He said to me why not try putting the Odaimoku first in my life and see how it goes. Try chanting first then do other things. He said that if you put the important things in your life first then they will get done and the other things will find their own place. In business today, one of the things successful people do is to continually focus on the most important objective and not allow themselves to be distracted.

In your life, what do you put first, what is your most important objective? If it is to become happy, to eliminate suffering, to establish a solid foundation for joy then the surest way is to chant Odaimoku. If other things come before chanting then you are not putting the important things in life first. Now maybe the truth of the matter is you have no real interest in attaining enlightenment, and that is your choice, but then you are not a Buddhist, because fundamentally being a Buddhist means you are striving to attain enlightenment.

The degree to which you devote yourself, or if you don't like the term devote then think of it as apply, or commit, or focus, or whatever, the degree to which you do this is the degree to which you will actually receive benefit. Your level of participation will determine the level of actual change to your life. There is no reward without effort.

I urge each of you to really make a determination from today to refocus your efforts, to really strive to practice daily and with a joyful heart knowing that what you are doing is certain to result in tremendous growth and change in your life.

When I first began practicing this Buddhism, when I first began chanting I was 19 years old. At that time I was encouraged to chant every day and to focus on not quitting and not slacking up for 10 years. At that time 10 years seemed like an impossibly long period of time. But I knew that I wanted to change my life and it was important to me. I also believed that by changing my life I could change the lives of others. I was in the military and very much opposed to war. I had a goal, you could say I had a life goal. It was important to me and I felt it was important to others. So I began my journey. Looking back over these past 45 years I can say that my life today is much greater than it would have been without Buddhism.

I really hope that you too can create a meaning filled life which you can look back on and say every moment was worth it. I promise you, if you set your mind to chanting every day, day in and day out, if you recite the sutra every day in ten years time you will be able to see a remarkable change in your life. And if you continue to do it throughout your life you will certainly attain a life of great joy and indestructible happiness.

This Lotus Sutra is the king of all the Buddha's teachings. Over an over in the Lotus Sutra the Buddha says that this teaching of his is the most important, and superior to all the other teachings he had taught before. He says the reason why he is teaching this great sutra is so that the people who believe in it, who revere it, and who uphold it are guaranteed to attain enlightenment equal to that of all the Buddhas throughout time.

I hope you keep this promise of the Buddha in your mind as you go through your life. I also hope that you consider carefully what it is you are devoted to, what is most important in your life, and then make sure your actions are in accord with your dreams. There is no greater dream than attaining enlightenment, hold that in your heart, in your mind and in your actions.

With Gassho,
Ryusho

Buddhism and Money

February 6, 2014 Dharma Talk

Today and every Thursday for the month of February I am going to write about finances, money, and wealth and how it all ties in to and can be thought about in terms of our Buddhist practice. The month of February is Financial Health in the United States, which is what originally gave me the idea.

Several years ago when I worked for Bank of America I would volunteer on Monday evenings teaching financial 'literacy' skills at Goodwill. Sometimes the group of students would be folks who were trying to start their lives over due to various setbacks they had suffered. At other times the groups were immigrants who were trying to start new lives in the United States.

The course was 10 weeks long and covered a wide range of subjects all dealing with finances and financial issues. Bank of America provided all the materials, though I was free to teach and structure the class in whatever manner I thought would be most beneficial to the students.

One thing that I found to be almost universal was that most Americans don't really understand money, and most of those who had come from other countries didn't understand credit, or not paying cash for something. Just because we practice Buddhism doesn't guarantee that we will be better equipped to handle finances. We bring the same things that troubled us in life before Buddhism into our Buddhist practice. If we don't actually apply any effort at making changes though we are likely to struggle with the same issues.

I am not an expert at all things financial and I am certainly not an expert at investment. I won't be making recommendations about how to invest or structure a savings portfolio, or making long-term financial decisions about retirement. I am not qualified to offer that kind of advice and that isn't really what I was thinking the purpose of this series would best accomplish. What I have in mind is more about basic concepts in finances, philosophy of money, some of the ways in which we are tricked into focusing on the wrong things when thinking about money, and some strategies about how we might bring Buddhism into that area of our lives.

Today to begin this series I would like to present to you a Money Meditation. I would like for you to consider this not as some cheap trick only to do one time, thinking it is cute and then forgetting about it. I propose that you make it a regular part of your practice, at least for a while. Perhaps since these posts will appear on Thursday you could make it a part of your Thursday practice. As with all things in life and certainly it is the case in Buddhism you will receive the most benefit if you actually make effort and do the practice.

I would like for you to remove from your wallet the highest denomination paper money you have. You might even consider getting a hold of high denomination paper bill and setting it aside just for these meditations. Please do this with the currency of your nation, so in the US it will be a dollar, in Europe it will be the Euro, in the UK it will be the pound, you get the idea.

To start with place along side of it a piece of paper currency that represents the lowest denomination of paper money. Now put both of those in front of you as you begin to practice. You can do this either as a silent meditation or you can begin chanting Odaimoku. As you are meditating, and remember chanting Odaimoku can be a meditation practice, consider these two pieces of paper. Ask yourself some of these questions and really think, ponder, and see if you can begin to feel deeply a response to the questions that perhaps goes beyond the words that come first to your mind. There is no right or wrong here, we are just going to explore your feelings.

Consider what the difference is between the two pieces of paper, what makes one worth more to society, to you, to a child who knows nothing about money, to someone from another country; what is it that has value and worth to you? What makes that piece of paper and an identical piece of paper of a different denomination mean the same thing to you as an accumulation of coins equal in value? Why is the paper worth the same to you and to society?

Now imagine if you will, and meditate on this, what if you lost a scrap of paper down the drain in the street. What would your feelings be? What are your feelings as you consider loosing the smaller denomination paper currency compared to the larger denomination currency? Are you still considering what it is fundamentally, the paper, and the ink?

Now finally look at the currency in detail. What does it look like, what is drawn on it, what are the markings on it, what pictures are on the currency? What does the paper feel like? What does the ink feel like, sometimes the currency is printed using an engraving process and the ink sits above the paper? Are there watermarks in the paper, or any special anti-counterfeit devices embedded in the paper? What color or colors are the inks? What are the differences between denominations? Really look and think about the currency in a non-monetary way.

I know I suggested doing this a minimum of once a week, however if you are able to do this more frequently it will be better and you will have a more significant experience as we expand this Money Meditation in future installments.

If you are able I suggest keeping a journal or diary of your thoughts, feelings, questions, observations. Also try to get into the habit of also including at least one gratitude. If you have any regrets make sure you have an equal number of gratitude items also listed. The number of regrets concerning money should not be greater than the number of thinks for which you are grateful.

Give this a try for the next seven days and we will pick this back up again next Thursday. See you then.
Now it's your turn. Please feel free to add your thoughts.

Buddhism and Money #2 – February 13, 2014

How did the Money Meditation go for you? Did you notice things about yourself you may not have been aware of before? Did you notice anything about money you had not considered before? Did you find your relationship with the pieces of paper change any? Perhaps nothing changed for you. There is no right or wrong here, there just is your awareness of yourself that is the most crucial thing.

Ponder this for a moment if you will. Say you are walking down the street and you see a penny on the ground. What do you do? Why do you do that? If you left the penny on the ground, what were your real reasons? Was it not worth your time since it was only a penny? Or did you leave it because it didn't belong to you?

Now imagine it was a dollar coin or a five-dollar bill. Did you leave it or did you pick it up? What were your reasons for doing whichever action you chose? If your actions changed between the two instances, what was the cause for your change?

If you were like most people you would leave the penny, mostly because it isn't worth your time to pick it up; it is only a penny. However as the denomination of the money increases the number of people who will pick up the money also increases. By the time it is a five-dollar bill or a twenty almost all people will pick it up.

It is interesting how money will change our actions and our motivations. It is also interesting how many excuses we are able to generate for not observing the precept of not taking what is not given to us, or not taking what is not ours.

Money is a very powerful thing indeed. But how powerful is it? I think that depends upon a variety of factors, one of which is certainly how great our need is or how great our desire is. But what is this thing we call money?

Fundamentally money is nothing other than a social contract we have entered into which says that something that is worth almost nothing we will treat as worth a great deal more. We agreed to assigned values for tokens, and these assigned values are supposed to be exchangeable for goods and services. We are paid with a token, which we can then exchange for a product. Everyone along the line agrees to honor the arbitrary value society has assigned, to what really amounts to an almost worthless piece of metal or paper.

Things used to be a bit different when precious metals or gems were used, as they at least had some rarity. Still however, the value was not fixed and was agreed upon by society, so there still was this social contract.

In the Lotus Sutra it is interesting to note the numerous references to wealthy individuals who were not royalty. In fact most of the parables are about working people or merchants. This reflects the rise in the merchant class both their rise economically, socially, and also the amount of influence they had on society. With this rise in the merchant class it became increasingly necessary to have more liquid forms of trading and acquiring wealth. Goods and services were moving in a multitude of directions, whereas previously wealth only moved within nobility or royalty.

In the Lotus Sutra we have stories of a wealthy man who has enough money to own a dilapidated house which we presume he didn't actually live in. Sadly his house caught fire, though his sons who were playing inside did escape. We had a merchant who wasn't always wealthy but managed to amass quite a fortune and he wanted to leave it to his son whom he hadn't seen in ages. We have the example of the son traveling around looking for work, so he was mobile even though no matter where he went he couldn't find work. We have a wealthy guy sewing gems in his friend's robe, neither of whom are nobility or royalty. We have a group of people who want to travel to another place because of economic opportunities. Before the rise of the merchant class people didn't move around so much because wealth tended to stay in one place.

History marches on and we come to ourselves. Today most people spend time at work producing only a part of a product, or even no real product at all. People work in factories or even fast food restaurants and perhaps only do one small part of the over all larger job. It may be a cashier who takes the order and collects the tokens which pay for the food someone else has prepared. Or it may the person sitting at a computer at a desk who manipulates information so the information can be then sold or utilized by someone they don't even know. Or, it might be what I used to do when I worked for the bank; moving what amounted to basically imaginary money around from one pocket to another thus creating false wealth (yes it was legal).

Money is time represented or effort represented by these arbitrary tokens we have assigned value to. So money has replaced our effort or time and made it something we can then give to someone else for different time or effort.

Our next part of Money Meditation is propose will be an active form of meditation. For this part of the meditation I would like for you to calculate how many minutes it takes you to earn one dollar (or what ever the lowest paper currency is in your country). Now firmly fix that in your mind so that you can easily calculate how much time it takes you to earn all of the various denominations of money you might come into contact.

One difficulty you will have with this meditation is the use of plastic cards such as charge cards or debit cards, because for many of us money doesn't even exist anymore. Even the arbitrary value we assigned to almost worthless tokens have been replaced by something that we haven't really adjusted to and has no set value.

OK, here is the actual mediation or practice. For the next week try to the best of your ability to translate the cost of the things you purchase, yes everything, into time spent earning the money you will spend. For those of us who don't make any money, or who are retired and living off money previously earned come up with a reasonable approximation. The real challenge will not be how much you actually make but doing the calculations.

I expect it to be tedious, and you may find yourself resisting doing it. Try to ask yourself why you might be resisting if you are. Is it too much trouble? Is it making you aware of the real cost of things? What are your feelings? And as you do it see if anything changes in you? Are you looking at things you buy in a different way? Are you considering the value or worth of something differently?

Benefits of Rituals

January 20, 2013 Dharma Talk

In Nichiren Shu, as well as in possibly all religions there are certain rituals that are performed as a part of the practice of that religion. Form some people these rituals can seem to be limiting. There may come times when we think to ourselves, why do we do the same thing over and over again; nothing seems to change, or it is boring why don't we do something differently.

In Buddhism we have a destination in mind as a reason for our practice. That destination is enlightenment. The Buddha revealed the destination through his own personal practice.

First he became aware of a reason for practice, that is to seek out a way to eliminate the sufferings of life. Next he realized that the answer was not to be found by continuing to lead a life of comfort and ease in the palace with his father. He abandoned his former life as a prince and set out to practice austerities in the forests. After several years of enduring harsh deprivations he sat beneath the Bodhi tree and became the awakened one we call the Buddha.

If we think of our Buddhist practice, the practice of attaining enlightenment, in terms of a guide and a traveler we can see that as a traveler we need to have a destination or goal in mind. Today when we wish to travel some place many people frequently reach for their GPS device and program in their destination then follow the directions provided. We think noting of doing this, it is ordinary, it is reasonable.

We do the same thing in our religious practice. We decide upon a destination, whether it is heaven or enlightenment. Then we find an appropriate GPS device and follow the directions provided.

In religious practice we replace our electronic GPS device with the instructions provided by previous travelers, such as teachers who have laid out a map for us to use as travel instructions.

"I once was attached to wrong views, and became a teacher of the aspirants for the teaching of Brahman. You expounded to me the teaching of Nirvana, and removed my wrong views because you understood me." (Lotus Sutra, Chapter III)

In Nichiren Buddhism our guides, our teachers are such people as Nichiren and others before him from which he drew upon when he studied. In other words they are teachers who have made a deep spiritual journey. Since the time of the Buddha they serve as our guide by outlining a way to practice a formula or ritual.

The ritual serves as an initial structure upon which we can build our own spiritual experience. We use ritual as a starting place, given to us so we do not have to start from scratch as we begin our practice. As time goes on we learn more and we can then expand upon the basic foundation that was given to us by our teachers.

It is much the same in many of life's endeavors. We might think of our practice as being in the world of action that helps us enter into the world of spirit. There is safety as we enter the world of spirit from action because there is a guide. When we lift weights, in order to do so we have a spotter someone who can assist us if we were to get into trouble. If it is scuba diving, sky diving, rock climbing, the list could be endless but in order to be safe, in order to gain the necessary expertise we seek out good teachers who will guide us as we learn our way.

Rituals can serve to open the window of opportunity, which is different from taking advantage of a window of opportunity already opened – the trick is that they open the window but they are not the window in itself. Rituals should and can serve to expand ones experience and transcendence – not limit them.

In our lives we rely on faith for many things. We have faith that the bridge we drive across will not collapse, we have faith in the buildings we inhabit or work in. We have faith in our cars. Faith is to some degree a relinquishing of control to those who have mastered the fine arts of the things we wish to participate in. The same goes for religion. We have faith in the teachers and the teachings and we realize that we may not have mastered all there is to know and we trust in teachers to instruct us.

Because you know all of the facts of something doesn't mean you have significantly changed your inner core of life. Having accumulated information does not equate to having made a significant advance in actualizing change. Ritual can help us transform information into actualization. Rituals can facilitate a transcendence from knowledge about something to actually manifesting the benefit of that knowledge.

"These people manifested by my supernatural powers will hear the Dharma from him, receive it by faith, follow it, and not oppose it." *(Lotus Sutra, Chapter X)*

As we chant the sutra and the Odaimoku we, even briefly, suspend our intellect to make space for the spirit to emerge and connect with the knowledge.

Spiritual Assessment

Written as part of my formal Chaplain certification

Working towards board certification as a professional chaplain requires, as part of the certification process, the development of a spiritual assessment tool. Each chaplain has to come up with their own tool, that fits their own unique style.

The tool serves multiple purposes, a couple of which I'll highlight here. One purpose is to assist the chaplain in making an assessment of where the patient is in their spiritual process around the particular crisis they are currently involved in. This isn't intended to measure the spirituality of the patient, but more to guide the chaplain in how to provide the best possible spiritual care appropriate for the healing of the patient.

Another use of the tool is to help the chaplain stay on track in the conversation. To assist the chaplain in ensuring that important areas of discussion are happening.

There are many different tools available that have been developed by chaplains over the years. Some revolve around different acronyms which facilitate in easy memorization. The goal is, however, for the chaplain to develop a tool that really suits their individual style of providing spiritual comfort. Mind you as chaplains our goal is not to proselytize or preach, it is to meet the patient wherever they are spiritually and assist them in an appropriate manner suitable to the patient to assist them in the time of crisis.

That care may or may not be of a particular religious tradition, sometimes it isn't even about religion at all. That is one of the differences between a chaplain and a pastor who comes to the hospital to visit a congregation member.

My journey over two plus years of training for certification has led me through several different assessment tools, and several evolutions of the same tool. Until recently I had adapted and fiddled with tools that other chaplains had used.

Several months ago, after reading a book about Buddhist Chaplains, it hit me that the most comfortable and most deeply aligned spiritual tool for me was at the heart of the Buddha's teachings of the Four Noble Truths.

I bring this to you today in this writing because I believe that this tool, while Buddhist in origin is universal in application and can be useful to anyone facing a crisis of any nature. I offer it to you for your own personal assessment.

Now I have taken some liberties with the Four Noble Truths and abbreviated them somewhat. But I see no harm in this and in fact makes it easier to apply in a much more general sense.

First, when faced with a problem, any problem, or crisis, is to correctly identify the nature of the problem. This is tricky sometimes as problems can be masked and hidden from us. So prayer, meditation, reflection are required sometimes to get to the root of the particular difficulty.

I work in heart units, primarily heart ICU and cardiovascular recovery, as well as a couple of cardiac units. A patient may present themselves in the hospital with a heart problem. In many ways that is only a symptom, a different approach from what a doctor might make where the heart issue is the problem that needs to be treated.

As a chaplain, one of my objectives in line with the hospital's mission of not just curing a patient but keeping them healthy my goal is to try to encourage the patient to participate in their health.

So, the heart may present as the problem, but usually there is something else underlying the issue. If this is a new heart problem then there will definitely need to be changes going forward.

So identify correctly the problem, just like your doctor would do. Next is the second noble truth which is to try to understand the cause of the problem. The doctor makes their diagnosis and prescribes a course of action. As the chaplain my role would be to get to some of the root behaviors that may have precipitated the heart crisis.

In your life, after you identify the cause of your particular problem, you would try to see if you can identify some of the causes for the problem.

Next would be to try to identify things that you can change that might result in different outcomes. For the heart patient, frequently it is being compliant in taking medications, proper diet, especially if there are issues complicating such as diabetes. And yes exercise is usually in there as well, even if now modified or limited due to the heart problem.

So you have identified the problem, gotten at some (maybe not all) the causes, and looked at things that could be done differently to result in different outcomes.

Now the Fourth Nobel truth is action. What action plans can you formulate that will encourage you or make it possible to make the changes you identified? For some people it may actually include something religious or spiritual as well as something physical.

There are many solutions or possible ways to change actions and many things that will support those changes or work against them. It is entirely up to the individual. My role as the chaplain is to help facilitate those changes, to open doors of possibility but primarily to assist the patient to come to their own answers.

This may not sound so spiritual, and yet it truly is a spiritual journey into the core of what living is. What does life mean to the patient, to you, to me? What does death mean to each of us? How valuable is this life to us and to what degree will we participate in living life, including how we draw upon our spiritual resources to assist in the physicality of life.

What are your methods of solving the crisis that inevitably arise in your life? I am curious to hear if you have a strategy that works for you.

Response to Questions About Inner Peace and Striving
July 7, 2013

The other day I received a response with a question about my post on inner peace, which appeared last week. Because that question is one I have heard or been asked several times in the past I thought I would just write a blog post about it. Because it is the sort of question that occurs somewhat frequently in one form or another I am posting it so that perhaps I can just post a link to the article next time it occurs. At any rate it is a good exercise for me to engage in and I ask your forgiveness if you think you need it.

Let me begin by saying that since this is my blog I am free to say what I want, and you the reader are free to disagree. Here I am going to exercise my prerogative of saying what I want. Please don't take this as me being snarky or flip. I mean this sincerely. What I post on this blog is mainly about my personal experience of practicing the Lotus Sutra in the Nichiren Shu tradition. It is my experience, which I hope can be used to inspire others to enjoy this Buddhist way. Since it is based on my experiences and my understanding it will not be universally or even infallibly true. It will be simply what it is.

The question I was asked sort of boiled down to a statement about the perception that Nichiren Buddhism is all about striving and what I said about inner peace was somehow in opposition to both. It was not a criticism of my post but of the perception of Nichiren Buddhism. The statement was followed with a question about whether what I said from my personal belief or from a "more orthodox Nichiren belief?" Examples offered to demonstrate the contradiction were their view that Nichiren Buddhism is about "a practice of striving (chanting, for example) and a practice for attaining "outer peace" (social engagement, peace protests, etc.)"

At this point I should say that I do not feel responsible for defending Nichiren Buddhism or the Lotus Sutra. I also am not responsible for any conclusions people formulate on their own and then hold up as a truth, either personal or universal. Everyone is entitled to their opinions, however they are acquired. Also I am not the final expert on all things Nichiren or Lotus Sutra. I am simply one person who tries to carry out the practice of the Lotus Sutra as taught by Nichiren.

So, first, as to the matter of striving, let me say all life is striving and all of living is striving. Simply put, the next breath you take will only be because at the base of your brain, the stem, a signal is being sent telling your lungs to breath. The muscles will exert an effort to cause your lungs to expand which in turn causes air to enter either your nose or your mouth; that is unless you are sitting there with a gaping hole in your chest.

If anyone thinks for even a moment that the Buddha did not strive, they are imagining a fairy tale Buddha, as real as every fairy tale. The Buddha was the Buddha because he strove. He stove to understand the way to eliminate the suffering of mankind. Once he became enlightened, he got up from the tree and strove tirelessly teaching his enlightenment. He stove endlessly until the day he died. To think otherwise, to think that Buddhism even exists today without striving or will continue to exist into the future without striving is to ignore the facts, the realities of Buddhism.

Inner peace and striving are not two contradictory states of being. The fault is that for us moderns we have come to think of striving as being an all out or nothing thing. Perhaps we might even confuse it with obsession and compulsion of acquiring things or of achieving success. The two are not the same; at least to me they are not.

Chanting Odaimoku is no more striving than sitting silently in meditation. Chanting Odaimoku is just another form of meditation and meditation is striving, to one degree or another. The trick is not to obsess or be compulsive. Either one done obsessively or compulsively is not practicing Buddhism. Bragging about how long one sits silently is no different than doing the same about chanting. Whether you sit or chant for 1 minute or for days is of no value to anyone not even yourself. The value is whatever value it had for you, not in the time it took. I have been practicing for over 40 years, and all I have to show is imperfection, so of what value is my 40 years to anyone.

Chanting or meditation can be a chore for anyone, it can also be equally liberating to anyone. So what is the difference? The only difference is the mind of the individual, and what limitations they are placing upon themselves; what hindrances are residing internally they are avoiding.

Buddhism is all about effort. It is Right Effort though. It is gentle, kind, consistent, middle way effort. Without any effort at all one would be left with almost none of the Eightfold Path which would shatter the Four Noble Truths. The Buddha exerted great, kind, loving, compassionate, selfless, unrelenting, effort so that we could become enlightened.

OK, so now on to the "outer peace". Some examples used were social engagement, peace protests, and "etc.". I am not sure what is to be included in "etc." hopefully it will be covered.

I would offer as a very pointed rebuttal the very example of the Buddha. The Buddha was very socially engaged. If he had not been we would not have Buddhism today. The difference perhaps is that the cause the Buddha involved himself in was the cause for all mankind to be able to eliminate suffering. Today others use Buddhism as a basis for their engagement in particular social causes such as world peace, or eliminating hunger, or struggling against social issues around homelessness, running hospice houses, or providing food to the hungry and on the list could go.

These kinds of efforts are not unique to Nichiren Buddhists, nor are they unique to Buddhism. As Buddhists we do not have a monopoly on social engagement, though I do feel we should be examples, especially is no one else is.

To not be socially engaged is to me to be less than human. If you look at the four lower worlds, they are all in a way sub human. They do not call upon the person to consider anyone other than self. The difference between the world of hunger and bodhisattva is that when sitting at the banquet table with a six foot fork the bodhisattva uses his fork to feed someone else and the person in hunger struggles to find a way to maneuver the six foot utensil into their own mouth.

One of the characteristics of the realm of humanity is the ability to consider others. If for a moment someone thinks that Buddhism is about living in the four lower worlds to the exclusion of the others, then they ignore the very reason Siddhartha gave up his worldly possessions, practiced austerities, gave up the selfish practice of austerities, ate porridge, sat under the tree battled Mara, and then got up from the tree and gave his life away selflessly to teach what he had attained. If the Buddha had never gotten up from the tree and stayed true to his original idea of sharing his enlightenment, the way to overcome suffering we would not have the luxury of any kind of Buddhist practice, either silent meditation or chanting.

Now, on to chanting. I won't belabor this because there is nothing new or unique about chanting. Chanting is practically if not absolutely a universal practice. I am not sure there has ever been a spiritual practice that at one point did not engage in chanting of some form or another. Even the military uses chanting and has since time beginning. Silent sitting, or what some people think is the only real form of mediation, has also been used probably in all spiritual practices. Buddhism is not unique in the value it places on any form of meditation.

What is probably unique, is that we moderns with our ever so clever, and arrogant minds waste our time debating what is the "best" or the "correct" way and so forth. We create a silly, no foolish, false dichotomy where one is and one is not, and pity the fool that choose the one we do not think is the absolute one.

Simply stated chanting is meditation. And both are possible to do and be of no value to the doer. You can waste as much time doing both or you can benefit, is up to the operator. The error is not in the operating system is in the user.

I think I am almost done here so if I still have your attention bear with me tad bit longer.

Regarding inner peace and outer peace. It has been my observation that if you don't have inner peace you really don't have outer peace. Yes I suppose a person could fake it but in the end I think the truth would be revealed. Fundamentally would you have outer peace if you had no inner peace? You might have an illusion of peace, but that is all it would be an illusion.

OK, this one last thing. Nichiren Buddhism is not such an aberration, as people would sometimes like to make it. Most of the time these kinds of assertions that somehow Nichiren Buddhism is some weird offshoot of Buddhism is more a round about way of trying to assert some superiority. In other words if they make one thing out to be inferior then they have crated a solid, in their mind solid, ground upon which to base their superior attitude.

There really isn't much about Nichiren that can't be found in others throughout the history of Buddhism. Nichiren taught his understanding of the Lotus Sutra. He did what he thought was best to enable common people to attain enlightenment by making it accessible and easy enough to practice. Yes he was socially engaged. There are many contemporary Buddhist leaders who are equally socially engaged maybe even more so, asserting even political power. No one, or not many, criticize them for being political and yet Nichiren, because he criticized the government of his time, is some how worth finding flaws and pointing them out.

Nichiren Buddhism is very much like any other Buddhism, the only real difference is we uphold the Lotus Sutra. Other Buddhist follow other sutras, or in the case of Chan Buddhism, no sutras. There are some American versions of Buddhism that have decided to abandon certain practices that have been a part of Buddhism and continue to be a part of Buddhism. In a way they might be the aberration, I'll leave that to each person.

I think fundamentally the problem is not the divisions of Buddhism but the ease with which we moderns can slide in to superior/inferior thought patterns. We moderns are such an arrogant bunch that we all too easily get on high horses and look down our noses at others. It really is a case of animality to the extreme. Animality is not the practice of Buddhism any more than the hunger I mentioned several hundred words ago.

If I were to boil all this down it would be simply that it is not accurate to think that in any way Nichiren Buddhism is not about inner peace. Nor is it accurate to think Buddhism does not include striving. The trick for each of us is, as I also said several hundred words ago, finding a true middle path.

Thanks for hanging around to the end. I have no prize to give to you, so if you were expecting one I can only ask, how does it feel to expect? Seriously, I hope you did not take offense at anything I have written. I only hope it is somehow a bit 'enlightening'.

With Gassho,
Ryusho

Ohigan and Equinox

September 22, 2013

Well, here we are approaching the autumn equinox. Twice a year on our planet we have an equinox, a period of equal light and equal dark. Twice a year we take time during the equinox season to pay particular attention to observing the Six Paramitas.

We find reference to Higan, which means crossing to the other shore, in the Lotus Sutra Chapter 1.

> *"They had already trained themselves out of their compassion towards others, entered the Way to the wisdom of the Buddha, obtained the great wisdom, and reached the Other Shore so that their fame had already extended over innumerable worlds."* Lotus Sutra, Chapter I

While it is true that every day and every moment are periods of transition. We are constantly in states of transition going from one thing to the next. Most of the time I am guessing we do so mindlessly until at some point we are aware we have done some thing or some period of time has elapsed. We may experience the same thing, especially at this time of year when we are reminded that the year is almost over.

The idea of crossing over to some other shore has some potential interesting images that can be conjured up. Of course one such image is of a ship that leaves one shore, travels across a body of water and finally drops anchor on a different shore. We could say that Buddhism is the ship that can carry us over the ocean of suffering. Early Mahayana Buddhists used the image of a ship or boat because it could transport many people.

Buddhism is like a ship traveling across the ocean of suffering is an easy image to think about. Yet, we would be somewhat lazy if we only thought of Buddhism as some comfortable cruse liner where we are passengers being transported in luxury and ease. In order to get the ship safely from one place to another there needs to be a highly organized crew to sail the ship. The crew needs to follow orders and do things in an orderly way.

The Six Paramitas you could say are like the rules and procedures for sailing a ship, sort of like the operating instructions. As the boat of Buddhism travels carrying people from one shore to another the journey is from ignorance to enlightenment; from dark into light. The equinox is a perfect time to think about the journey from dark to light and the equality of both. An interesting thought about life is there is an equal potential for joy as there is for suffering.

If you consider the realm of humans to be relatively neutral; neither great suffering nor great joy, then there are four realms that are lower and four realms that are higher. We have at any moment of time an equal potential to experience joy or suffering, the thing that will decide matters is our faith and practice. The basic practice guidelines, or instructions for life, are the Six Paramitas, along with chanting the Odaimoku. In the realm of humanity we are in a sense in an equinox equivalent of state of mind. If we abandon our practice and our faith then we will gradually find our condition of life slowly on a downward spiral potentially. Yet if we renew our practice and determination we can slowly improve our life condition. We can, through our practice of Six Paramitas cross over to the other side of enlightenment.

In our lives we continually come up against equinox moments where depending upon the thing we choose the future will be dramatically different. Sometimes they are easy to spot, even if not easy to decide. Other times the transition moment may be not so easy to spot, it could be as simple as choosing to say a word in anger or reframing from responding.

It is as if we are on the boat of Buddhism making our way to a shore, the challenge then becomes which shore we will choose to debark upon. Will we choose to debark on one shore to embark on a new journey with different skills as our tools. Will we use the Six Paramitas, the Lotus Sutra, and Odaimoku to ensure our path is one of joy. Or will we abandon our practice turn around mid-journey and debark from the boat of Buddhism onto the shore we originally started from. Will we in our equinox moments choose a path of change illuminated by Buddhist practice, or will we fall back into unskillful practices and ensure ourselves of a life of repeated sufferings.

During these days of Ohigan around the fall equinox, I hope you will renew your focus on adopting the Six Paramitas as a foundational set of principals on which to live your life.

He Has Destroyed Villages and Towns- Everyone is Frightened of Him
September 8, 2013

Good morning, thank you all for joining with us here at the temple today to practice together the Lotus Sutra. It isn't easy to practice even a little bit of the Lotus Sutra in this modern age. In Chapter 15 of the Lotus Sutra, among other places in the sutra, the Buddha tells us in many different ways how difficult practicing the Lotus Sutra would be in the time after his death. Because it is so difficult, the merit accumulated from our efforts is much greater than any other way of practicing Buddhism. Alongside the Buddha's words explaining the difficulty of practicing the Lotus Sutra are his words extolling the great benefit of actually overcoming the difficulties to practice.

Here we are today just a few days away from the anniversary of the spectacular and deadly attack on the Twin Towers in New York City. Like the assassination of President John Kennedy, September 11 will be a marker day in people's lives. People will be able to recall what they were doing, where they were and all sorts of details on those marker days.

One of the activities that mark this anniversary for me is to speak about terrorism and retaliation or revenge, and the cycle it puts into motion. The perfect example in Buddhism for teaching on the harm of retaliation, revenge, or retribution is given to us in the story of Angulimala; the most famous terrorist. Angulimala was a serial murderer who would kill his victims, cut off their fingers and wear them strung on a necklace around his neck. Angulimala translates as finger necklace. You might recognize the word mala in his name, mala is what we call our prayer beads, though in Japanese it is called juzu. But mala is the widely used term throughout the Buddhist world.

The story of Angulimala is not a simple one. It begins with the child Angulimala being an outcast, a member of the caste of untouchables whom society would have nothing to do with. Through no fault except birth this person was reviled by society. His parents tried to raise him to accept his position in life and get on with life. How many times has a line similar to that been used even here in our own country.

We expect the lowest in our society to accept their place, to somehow magically against overwhelming odds and with little support to somehow transform their lives, as if the majority ever had to do the same themselves. The fact is that most of the majority if not all of the majority population in our society has never come close to challenging society in ways African-Americans have or in the ways that many immigrants have. Yes true, some Caucasian people have been poor and improved their lives, but they had a leg up, they were the same color as the society in which they were trying to move up in.

Yes there are examples of many people of color, of all the colors, having improved their lot in life, but often the truth is they have just barely improved their social status but not made a dent in the general prejudices that they are still confronted with just because of the color of their skin. There is nothing more frightening to the core psyche of a white man than a black man with a gun, we saw examples of this in the 60's and it still exists today. Yet a white man with a gun is somehow not supposed to be feared.

Before I get to far down stream let me bring it back to Angulimala. He, in anger, left his home because he could not tolerate the horrible existence his family and society was trying to impose on him. In anger he decided that his only power available was to become so fearsome people and thereby control their emotions.

The Buddha, according to the story goes out in search of this terrorist Angulimala, even as he continues to kill and is hunted by the forces of the king. The Buddha in the midst of this reign of terror and the authoritarian response plants his life in the middle so that he can save not only the people Angulimala is killing but to save Angulimala himself. The image that comes to mind when I recount this story is that of Thich Nhat Hanh who during the Vietnam War would gather up other Buddhist monks and walk between the enemy lines carrying large flags.

Walking a path of hate and revenge is an easy path to walk, and it will always be populated with plenty of fellow travelers, though the destination remains elusive to all who travel that road. There is no peace or security that is long lasting by practicing the easy practice of hatred, revenge, and retribution. It is an endless cycle that regenerates itself.

For the entire history of man we have example after example of the pointless engagement in revenge or the use of force to overcome force. Hatred breeds hatred, violence breeds violence. The examples I could give would cause your eyes to glaze over and walk away.

In the book The Buddha and the Terrorist by Satish Kumar the Buddha says to Angulimala, "The power of the sword is dependent on the weakness, submission and powerlessness of others. The power of love empowers everyone: it is self-organizing and self-sustaining. All beings, human and other than humans, are naturally equipped with this intrinsic power and it is released through the relationship of mutuality; reciprocity, friendship, and love. All efforts of control over and conflict with others end in tears, frustration, disappointment – or war."

Today, the message I would like for each of us to try to really embrace is that all of our actions result in consequences, both as individuals and as society. As we think about our actions and what actions we wish our government to engage in which do we choose? Do we go with the easy to follow path of power over, of revenge, or retaliation, of retribution, of hatred and killing, which only generates more of the same? Or do we follow a more difficult path a path that by its very nature of being in opposition to force is fraught with peril, but one which ultimately yields the results we truly seek, that of peace.

In the story of Angulimala because of the risk the Buddha took, this person, Angulimala, is self-reformed and becomes a great teacher of Buddhism, able to explain the difficult and complex theories of Buddhism to even the most common person. I encourage you to get a copy of this small book and read for yourself. By the way the title of today's Dharma talk is a quotation from this book: The Buddha and the Terrorist, by Satish Kumar.

With that I close today with a prayer of safety and happiness of each person today, even any enemies I may have or may have caused. I pray the same for our country and for all the peoples of the world. May we all make great effort not only for our individual happiness but for the happiness of every person, even those we find easy to hate.

No Temple, What Do I Do

August 11, 2013

It is lamentable there are not more Nichiren Shu Buddhist temples in America or the world. It is lamentable there are not more Buddhist Temples of any kind in America. Very few cities or town have Buddhist temples accessible to practitioners. There is a solution though, sadly too many people find it easier to lament and do nothing living in a delusion and trying to create an illusion that somehow it is someone else's fault, or that someone else should fix it.

It really is easy to have a Nichiren Shu temple in your community. There are a number of ways to make it possible for you to have close access to a priest or Sangha center.

One way is to take 8-10 years out of your life, train and study and become ordained. It shouldn't be hard for you to do that, you just need the time and money. But mostly you need a real desire, a heart for Buddhism, and the self realization that our practice is not just for ourselves it is for other people to become happy and escape from suffering.

If that doesn't suit you, and becoming a priest is not the path for everyone, nor should it be. There is another way though. Simply work with others in your community to collect donations to pay the salary for a priest who has dedicated their time, money, and effort to receive training. Of course you will need to provide a place for practice so either buying or renting a building will be necessary, not too terribly difficult.

None of those are impossible, there are several Nichiren Shu priests in America who have done that.

I have found though over the years that mostly people want to complain and do nothing, or to create expectations for others to fulfill without really making any effort themselves.

One such example of this is this blog. Over the past year I have not been able to put up new content on a regular basis. The reason for that is due to me taking 3 years out of my life to further my training so there would be one more Buddhist Chaplain in America and a single one in my community. I do believe that my efforts are in line with living my life dedicated to the spread of Buddhism.

Right now the daily average for page views on this blog is between 40 and 50 views a day. When I was creating new content on a daily basis, the count was 150 or more a day. The really strange thing is though, no one makes any donation to the temple, and yet they freely come and take advantage of the services offered. Strange.

Now if the content was not appreciated by anyone then you would expect that viewers would eventually trickle off to almost none. Yet even with content that isn't being constantly replenished and refreshed there are still at least 40 views a day, every day. People come, they read, many probably come back, and yet there are no donations.

Right now there is one person who almost never makes a complaint that there is no temple near him. He works very hard, long hours and supports two children and his wife. I imagine he makes perhaps average income, yet for most people average isn't really enough. Yet this person at least once a week, sometimes several times a week makes a donation through Pay Pal of a few dollars. Sometimes it is more sometimes it is less. It isn't necessarily the amount of his donation that is remarkable or praiseworthy, it is the fact that he constantly does this. Not just recently but for several years now.

Yet most people come, they take, and they donate nothing. How does that really equate to supporting or even really making effort to have a temple in their community? If there is no support for what is available then how is it going to be possible to have something more?

I am not the only priest who experiences this. I hear from other priests who get email or communication complaining that the services that are streamed are interrupted by advertisements, or that they aren't recorded for viewing at some more convenient time. And yet, there are no donations for that, yet there is the expectation the offerings from priests and temples should be greater.

Virtually none of the new Nichiren Shu temples has any steady reliable income on which to budget any expansion of services. This temple is virtually supported by one person, me the priest. What little donation that comes in doesn't cover much, and there is nothing left to save for the future. So when I quit supporting it, it will vanish. This temple is not the only one.

Nothing comes cheaply or free. If you don't believe me try it yourself.

Buddhism isn't about money, society is about money and Buddhism exists within the context of society. Temples exist within the context of and under the requirements of society. All of those requirements and contexts cost money. Buildings cost money. Electricity costs money. Water costs money. Food costs money. Altars cost money. Training to become a priest costs money. If you don't like that then work to change it, as many priests are currently doing.

Ask yourself as you read this content and others on this web page, when was the last time I made a donation to this temple to support this effort you are partaking of? It doesn't need to be much, a couple of dollars. But it does need to happen and it needs to be regular. If it isn't Buddhism will grow very slowly if at all noticeably.

Even if you don't want a temple and want to practice on your own think of what it still costs you to do that? If you want it to grow then at the least it will take opening up your life, perhaps your home, most likely your wallet, to make it possible for others to practice.

If you are still reading by this point, let me say, that this is not some angry burnt out priest responding. I enjoy doing what I do. I have willingly dedicated time, money, and effort so that I could fulfill my personal desire to act according to my belief in the Lotus Sutra and desire to fulfill the Buddhas teaching of spreading the Dharma to others. But I am fully qualified to call B.S. to the illusion that the lack of a temple in a person's community is somehow someone else's responsibility. I am fully qualified to call B.S. to the delusion that somehow that is anything other than a selfish misguided attempt to call one's practice anything other than selfish (for one's personal gain).

Now it is fine if people want to live under their own delusion, but that isn't what Buddhism is about. We are striving to live free from delusion and illusion. I will help you do that, buy not participating in either of them on your behalf. Just think about this, if you get mad, quit reading the blog, go someplace else, or what ever whose life does it affect? Please don't think it affects anyone else's but your own.

It is my hope though that by this point you will have generated a spark within your life to find it possible to make a donation to this temple and to continue to do so. I will continue to do my best to support your Buddhist practice and your growth of faith in the Dharma of the Lotus Sutra. I can tell you that in Buddhism there is really no wasted effort. Your donations while in the immediate sense help ensure the continuation of Buddhism, but in a greater sense they create within you and your life greater fortune. Gratitude is the easiest way to expand your life, giving does not contract your life it causes it to grow and become large to gain more fortune.

Thank you for reading this and for your support.

With Gassho,
Rysuho, Shonin

Four Sufferings
Birth
March 4, 2014

"The triple world is not peaceful.
It is like the burning house.
It is full of sufferings.
It is dreadful.
There are always the sufferings
Of birth, old age, disease and death.
They are like flames
Raging endlessly."
Lotus Sutra, Chapter III

Traditionally there are four things given as sufferings of life. The four are variously given as birth, old age, disease or sickness, and finally death. Today, and for the following three Tuesdays, I will write about these four sufferings.

Recently on an email group list the question came up about whether or not birth was such a bad thing, and didn't we need to be born in order to carry out our Bodhisattva practice to save all beings. A distinction I would like to make here is concerning the idea of birth being either good or bad, and separating it from an understanding of it being directly related to suffering.

I think if you ask most people birth is a good thing, especially for the parents of a newborn child. On the other hand a birth might be an unwelcome event, depending upon circumstances. This value of good and bad is too subjective, and potentially misleading when we are talking about causes for suffering.

Suffering in itself is merely suffering, and is a fact of life. The First Nobel Truth speaks to this very subject. I believe that what Buddhism helps us to understand is for every action that occurs there is a potential for suffering. When we understand this we can actually begin to free ourselves from much of the effect of suffering and when it occurs we are less likely to respond to that suffering in ways that will increase the suffering.

I sometimes will talk about it in terms of a contract, a contract where there is a clause, which says 'something may go wrong and things may not work out or last forever'. This is not a part of the reality of life we are comfortable looking at or even acknowledging. Yet it is always there. It is there when we get in our car in the morning and go to work, it is there when we fall in love, it is there when a new life is brought into the world. We choose to ignore it for a variety of reasons, not the least of which, it is a terribly pessimistic way to live and just the reality can create fear and consequently more suffering.

Let's look at birth today. I am guessing that most people when they think of birth in this context they think about a newborn baby, so let us start there. I know a chaplain who talks about the terror or trauma of birth for the baby. Here is this baby who is living in this perfect climate controlled, water-cushioned environment where food is automatically supplied, and there is a waste management system included. Life in this environment is just about perfect for the infant. Finally on birth day the baby is ejected from this perfect environment into a cold room full of bright lights and people, perhaps lots of people.

The baby soon realizes that its water cushioned ride no longer exists and it also realizes that if it wants nourishment it will need to do something to have its needs met. Things just got extremely complex for this helpless life form. The trauma of birth sets into motion a life that until death is one of trying to manipulate life in such a way that will allow it to survive, joy and happiness are potential by products of this experience but certainly not priorities. Survival is the single most important thing for life. Yes different life forms have the ability to exhibit compassion and self-sacrifice but those only come later and under select circumstances.

Birth in itself is an event that begins with trauma, but that trauma does not reflect whether or not there is suffering. In fact I suspect that the concept or experience of suffering distinct from pain doesn't develop until much later in life. I'm not an expert in child development but this is what I suspect to be the case.

Now let us consider birth in other ways. Every day we are born again to a new day of new experiences. Yes, they are new, even if they are like other experiences in previous days. Every day begins again, and every moment begins again. In a way our entire life is defined by birth, unceasing, and unrelenting. Because we have done it so many times in our lives we don't give it much thought, but it is there none the less. Every moment we begin again. All of the security of having survived to this moment is gone and the struggle for survival begins again, since nothing is guaranteed in life and nothing lasts forever, even if the odds are that nothing will change, they could.

We also give birth to new ideas and new projects for our lives. This birthing of ideas can be exciting or it can be scary, it depends upon the individual. Frequently though the birthing of ideas is a cause for hope and excitement, though certainly not always. As new ideas are born within us they are also safe, because the do not need to meet any expectations of performance or success. Once they have been born and launched into the world though it can be very challenging to keep them alive.

There are, as you can see many ways in which to consider birth. As to whether or not birth is a good or bad thing is a value we attribute to the event, and purely individually subjective. But birth is indeed a cause of suffering simply because along with that birth, any birth, there is that clause in the contract which states 'it may not last, it may not succeed, it will not remain unchanged'. Also keep in mind that suffering is not necessarily a bad thing or something to be avoided.

Suffering, when we understand the nature and cause can become a fertile place to grow and nurture our enlightened life. It is when we become stuck in the suffering or when we proceed in unskillful ways that suffering is less than desirable. Becoming a victim to our suffering leads to more suffering, as does acting in unskillful ways. Suffering is not something to be avoided, since it really can't be avoided any way.

Birth as a potential source of suffering is a fact. It isn't a bad thing, nor good, it simply is, it is neutral. What we do with the effect, which has been caused, is the key to becoming happy and enlightened.

Next week I'll post about 'old age' and it may not be what you are thinking about.

Four Sufferings
Disease
March 18, 2014

"The triple world is not peaceful.
It is like the burning house.
It is full of sufferings.
It is dreadful.
There are always the sufferings
Of birth, old age, disease and death.
They are like flames
Raging endlessly."
Lotus Sutra, Chapter III

In this installment I will cover the suffering of disease. Generally when we use the term disease we think first of sickness of the body. However, now you might perhaps be thinking of the way many things become diseased, especially since in this series I have been showing how these four sufferings apply to many things other than just our bodies which can also cause us suffering.

Dis-ease is the way one of my Chaplain instructors would say the word in order to emphasize the fact that there is no long ease present in the person. Disease is not one condition but many types of conditions which all result in some malfunction or breakdown of the body which can cause either physical or emotional crisis. Disease is generally not planned, coming to each of us unexpectedly, and it is usually not welcomed.

Over these past few articles and in recent other blog postings I have talked about interconnection and disease is usually something that does not just affect one person but groups of people. These groups of people may simply be family members or they may be entire societies, and they also impact those trained professionals who help people overcome disease.

Disease affects not only people though, it affects animals, it affects social structures, it affects governments, it affects economies, it affects ideas.

Everything that can ever be born is subject to disease, including religions and their beliefs or practices.

The Buddha teaches in the Lotus Sutra that over time it would become increasingly more difficult to practice Buddhism because it would be corrupted with false ideas and misleading teachers thereby making it difficult just to sort out what teaching would be the most efficacious for the people of certain eras to practice. In other words Buddhism too would suffer disease and if not rescued it would potentially die. The Lotus Sutra is the teaching he intended to rescue Buddhism in ages when Buddhism is declining.

I work with the sick and dying as I carry out my Chaplain responsibilities, and in that process I work with doctors and nurses who provide medicines and prescribe treatments for those who are diseased. These treatments are intended to enable the individual to recover to the point where that person is capable of taking care of their own health.

The good medicine of the Lotus Sutra acts in much the same way. The Buddha has given the prescription to treat the disease of the degeneration of Buddhism in the form of the Lotus Sutra. It is the good medicine he left us but it is only going to be effective if we consume that good medicine by actually carrying out the practices of faith, study, reading, reciting, and teaching others.

In the parable of the Good Physician we have the children who are suffering from some poison they have consumed, they are said to be diseased of the mind. They are incapable of making good choices and so some refuse the perfect medicine, it is a medicine which is perfect in color, fragrance, taste and it ability to cure. The Lotus Sutra is just like that medicine, being perfect in all ways to measure a medicine, and it is capable of curing the most fundamental disease of delusion.

I have been working as a Chaplain for over three years now and I witness an interesting phenomena, something all healthcare professionals see as well; frequent readmissions for the same or similarly related diseases. In other words the same people come in for the same things repeatedly. Most often these are fully treatable conditions and have been treated in the past except the individual after being treated and healed fails to participate in their own continued good health. Eventually and frequently these same people either die or will die from this repeated condition; something that is completely treatable but requires patient participation.

Our Buddhist practice is like this as well. In order for this good medicine to cure us of our disease of delusions and enable us to break the cycle of suffering we need to not only take the good medicine it is also necessary to begin to participate in our own good spiritual health.

When people first come to practice Buddhism frequently they will notice a rapid change in their lives; perhaps even overcoming some obstacle or problem that has plagued them. This provides some immediate relief and there is a feeling of joy and happiness. Then however the critical time arises when they either reach a plateau of relative peace and security or they reach a really difficult patch in their lives. It is at this point when many people choose to abandon their practice.

This is very similar to those people who are frequently readmitted into the hospital for the same illness which are preventable. The way to end suffering is available to us through our daily practice of the Lotus Sutra though chanting the Odaimoku and reciting passages of the Sutra. This is much the same as following dietary guidelines or exercise programs in order to maintain good health. The daily practice of the Lotus Sutra is the prescription to maintain good spiritual health.

I hope you will continue in your daily practice so that you will be able to create a strong spiritual foundation for the blossoming of your enlightened life.

Four Sufferings
Old Age
March 11, 2014

"The triple world is not peaceful.
It is like the burning house.
It is full of sufferings.
It is dreadful.
There are always the sufferings
Of birth, old age, disease and death.
They are like flames
Raging endlessly."
Lotus Sutra, Chapter III

Having covered birth we now move to old age. Sometimes when explanations of these sufferings is given there is another step included which covers growth before old age. I think that as I write about old age I will include growth as well, because there is certainly potential for suffering as well.

Traditionally it is taught that the first sermon of the Buddha was the Four Noble Truths the first of which is the truth that there is suffering. The following three noble truths depending upon how they are translated can lead a person to think that the Buddha was teaching us a way to completely avoid any suffering in life at all. I think this would be a misunderstanding and a misleading way to ever interpret the Buddha's most important message.

I think what the Buddha sets out to do is first to recognize that suffering is simply a fact of our very existence. The Buddha lost his mother during child his own birth. In spite of the purported lavish and luxurious lifestyle the Buddha's father heaped upon his son, nothing could remove the fact that by his very birth the Buddha lost his mother, and the complicated grief dynamics that potentially sets in motion. The Buddha lived his whole life possibly wondering about the mother he never had.

No matter what we do as living human beings we will always be susceptible to suffering, it is as the Buddha teaches simply a fact of life. What the Buddha set out to accomplish I think was how do we manage, how do we respond to, and how do we live with that very reality. Suffering causes emotions and how do we ensure that our emotional response, either negatively or positively, does not either complicate the suffering or even lead to more suffering.

After birth, whether it is a baby, or a new idea, or a job, or a brand new car there ideally is a period of perhaps some growing pains or even some relative calm and stability. I have never raised a baby so all of my information is via third parties, but I have heard that babies are constantly changing, they are growing, they are learning, and they are pooping. And they just keep growing until they eventually grow up to be fully independent beings capable of living on their own after roughly 18-20 years of eating parents out of house and home and causing untold grief either as rebellious teenagers or perhaps some other act of separation from the family nest.

Of course I remember some of this as a first hand experience of the rebellious part, of the leaving home part and establishing my own life; thankfully I did not have to experience it from my parents perspective, and for that I must express gratitude to my parents for putting up with what they did.

Ideas frequently have a similar trajectory, a new club or organization, or a new business; new restaurants frequently have rocky births. Then after things get going they may settle down some and achieve a certain amount of stability, though not always. Sometimes right after conception and birth things deteriorate rapidly and become 'old' perhaps nearing death.

I have known restaurants that have had a grand launch and then three weeks later you can already feel the life has gone out and the place is on its last legs, even when the food was perfectly good. The demise or the old age of the business may have been caused by poor planning, or poor management, or just simply because it happens.

Old age is not simply a collection of wrinkled skin or a bag of frail bones. While it is that it is also about ideas and attitudes, it is about the afternoon and early evening of the day, it is about the third quarter in a game sometimes, it is about the failure of a business to adapt it's product to changing technologies and slowly becoming obsolete.

Old age is many outward experiences but it is also an inner journey and experience as well. It is about a person realizing that things done as a teenager or early adolescent are either not possible or not completely appropriate; the time has passed. Old age is about realizing there are other more appropriate activities to engage in such as processing knowledge into wisdom to be passed down to future generations. Old age is an inner journey into both preparing to let go of life, but also to experience the joys of life from a completely new perspective unencumbered by the pressure of the achievement driven youth.

Old age can be both scary and exciting, whether viewed as some event outside our life or as something to do with our life. It is not an easy journey regardless and there is the struggle with suffering constantly present just as suffering is present in growth. As we grow up towards old age the suffering is perhaps the fear of failure. In old age it is the fear of letting go, and the fear of death.

In all of these, suffering is a fact of our very existence, not to be avoided. We only cause ourselves more suffering is we think there is some way to magically escape entirely from suffering. What I believe Buddhism teaches us though, and I base this not just on theory but also on some personal life experience as I move into old age, what Buddhism teaches is a way to manage suffering, a way to experience suffering through truth. Buddhism teaches us a way to move into suffering with grace and strength and courage knowing that just as happiness is not without end so too is suffering and so we proceed through life in all situations making the causes that will cause us the least amount of further suffering.

Next week we get to talk about disease, something I witness almost every day in the hospital.

Four Sufferings
Death
March 25, 2014

Finally we come to the really big bugaboo for all living beings. Death is the single life event that for many brings the most fear and suffering. Death comes to us all, yet it is the most mysterious for what we do not know about death and especially what comes afterward. Death is the subject for which all the experts on it are dead.

Though I could be wrong, it is my belief that death is the fundamental reason for all religions, and the single thing that possibly all religions have the least amount of empirical evidence to support whatever belief it proposes. I once had a Chaplain supervisor ask me why I was so calm about death and dying when Buddhism has the least to offer when it comes to dying.

By this he meant there is no promise of some beautiful afterlife. As a Christian himself he said that it is interesting that with a beautiful promise of an afterlife where there are no worries or concerns and where all things are answered and all the troubles of life are eliminated it was something that most were unwilling to experience.

Even with a promise of a wonderful afterlife many people are very much afraid of what comes next

Let Us Not Be Twigs and Leaves
Paris, France
March 1, 2014

Good evening to you all, thank you for joining together tonight to chant the Lotus Sutra and the Sacred Title, the Odaimoku of Namu Myoho Renge Kyo. I feel so fortunate to be among you all tonight. Though we do not speak each other's language we could transcend that difference as we recited the Expedient Means and Life Span Chapters together in the Shindoku.

Tonight gathered here are Nichiren practitioners who may belong to different Nichiren groups, I think this is a wonderful experience. Not only do we not all share the same language, we also have different approaches to understanding and putting into practice the teachings of our founder Nichiren Shonin. On many levels we are able to transcend our differences for the sole purpose of praising the Lotus Sutra and holding it supreme above minor differences.

In Chapter XV 'The Appearance of Bodhisattvas From Underground' Chapter in the Lotus Sutra we are told of the emergence of many Bodhisattvas who suddenly rise up from the ground after having lived in the sky below the earth. This is a strange and shocking event witnessed by the great assembly gathered around the magnificent stupa of Many Treasures hovering in the sky.

We are told these great Bodhisattvas had the thirty-two marks of a Buddha, they were golden-colored, and they emitted innumerable rays of light. These are just a few of the descriptions of what these great Bodhisattvas looked like. We are also told how they arrived in various groups, with various followers, and attendants. The size of this great group of Bodhisattvas is beyond counting.

I have mentioned this many times in the past, however I will mention it again because I think it is important and demonstrates the mind of these great Bodhisattvas. Unlike others in the gathered assembly who had all asked the Buddha to predict their future enlightenment, these Bodhisattvas asked nothing of the Buddha except inquiring about his well being, his health, and his ease or difficulty of teaching the Dharma.

I believe that those of us who are practicing the Lotus Sutra today, both here in this place and all over the world, any one who chants the Odaimoku is capable of manifesting all the characteristics and benefits of the great Bodhisattvas who arose from the ground. Because we are all Bodhisattvas who are carrying out the practice of the Lotus Sutra, and who are trying to teach and spread this great teaching of the Buddha should we not all unite?

I believe that it is possible for us to spread the Dharma of the Lotus Flower Sutra even in our different ways and still be united in the cause to establish a peaceful society. We may have different approaches, and different ways of understanding the Lotus Sutra, but we are all striving towards the same objective.

I will be honest with you. I do believe that what I understand about the Lotus Sutra supports the acceptance of many different ways to approach the sutra all with the single practice of chanting the Odaimoku. I know there are those who disagree and who think that only they have the absolute correct way to understand the Lotus Sutra.

Those who think that only they are correct and turn their backs on or ridicule or disrespect other practitioners of the Lotus Sutra, are in fact acting like the five thousand who got up and left in Chapter II whom the Buddha called arrogant, and said they only think they have obtained something which in fact they have not. He said they were the sticks and leaves and to let them go.

So, for those who are unwilling to cooperate with other Nichiren Buddhists who sincerely chant the Odaimoku and work to spread the Lotus Sutra I say let them be and let us move on and gather those great Bodhisattvas who will join together as the many and varied Bodhisattvas from beneath the ground and spread this great and wonderful teaching of the Lotus Sutra.

Let us chant together with the Nipponzan Myohoji followers, let us chant together with Rissho Kosei Kai, let us chant together with Reiyukai practitioners, let us chant together with the independents, and let us chant with the Soka Gakkai if they wish to join and Nichiren Shoshu practitioners and Kempon Hokke Kai. I believe it is going to take all of us in our many and varied approaches to reach the greatest number of people throughout the world.

In fact at Mount Minobu you will see many different groups of practitioners who are not Nichiren Shu come to Kuon-ji temple and chant together. The hills and valleys of the Minbou complex and town are filled with the sounds of people from all over who come and march, beat drums, and chant Odaimoku. I have marched with the Nipponzan Myohoji practitioners chanting the Odaimoku. I will not turn away anyone, even if I am turned away. I believe it is time we challenge ourselves to put into practice not only with people outside of Nichiren Buddhism but people inside as well, that we follow the example of Bodhisattva Never Despise Fukyo and respect all believers.

Let me close by sharing with you this quote from the Lotus Sutra.

"If you see anyone who keeps, reads and recites the Sutra of the Lotus Flower of the Wonderful Dharma in the later five hundred years after my extinction, you should think, 'Before long he will go to the place of enlightenment, defeat Mara and his followers, attain Anuttara-samyak-sambodhi, turn the wheel of the Dharma, beat the drum of the Dharma, blow the conch-shell horn of the Dharma, send the rain of the Dharma, and sit on the lion-like seat of the Dharma in the midst of the great multitude of gods and men."
Lotus Sutra, Chapter XXVIII

Thank you all for joining with me here in France tonight. I hope that as each of you returns to your home that you will be cautious, get rest and stay healthy. Let us all work together to spread the great teaching of the Lotus Sutra far and wide all over the earth.

With Gassho,
Ryusho Shonin

Connect with Ryusho Jeffus on-line:

Twitter:
@ryusho @myoshoji

Facebook:
https://www.facebook.com/Ryusho

Facebook Author Page:
https://www.facebook.com/revryusho

Blog:
https://www:ryusho.org/blog

Amazon Author Page
https://tinyurl.com/y6z9rcbm

Made in the USA
Middletown, DE
26 May 2021